ADVANCE CLOUD COMPUTING

CLOUD COMPUTING

RAHUL SHARMA

ISBN 979-888606541-1

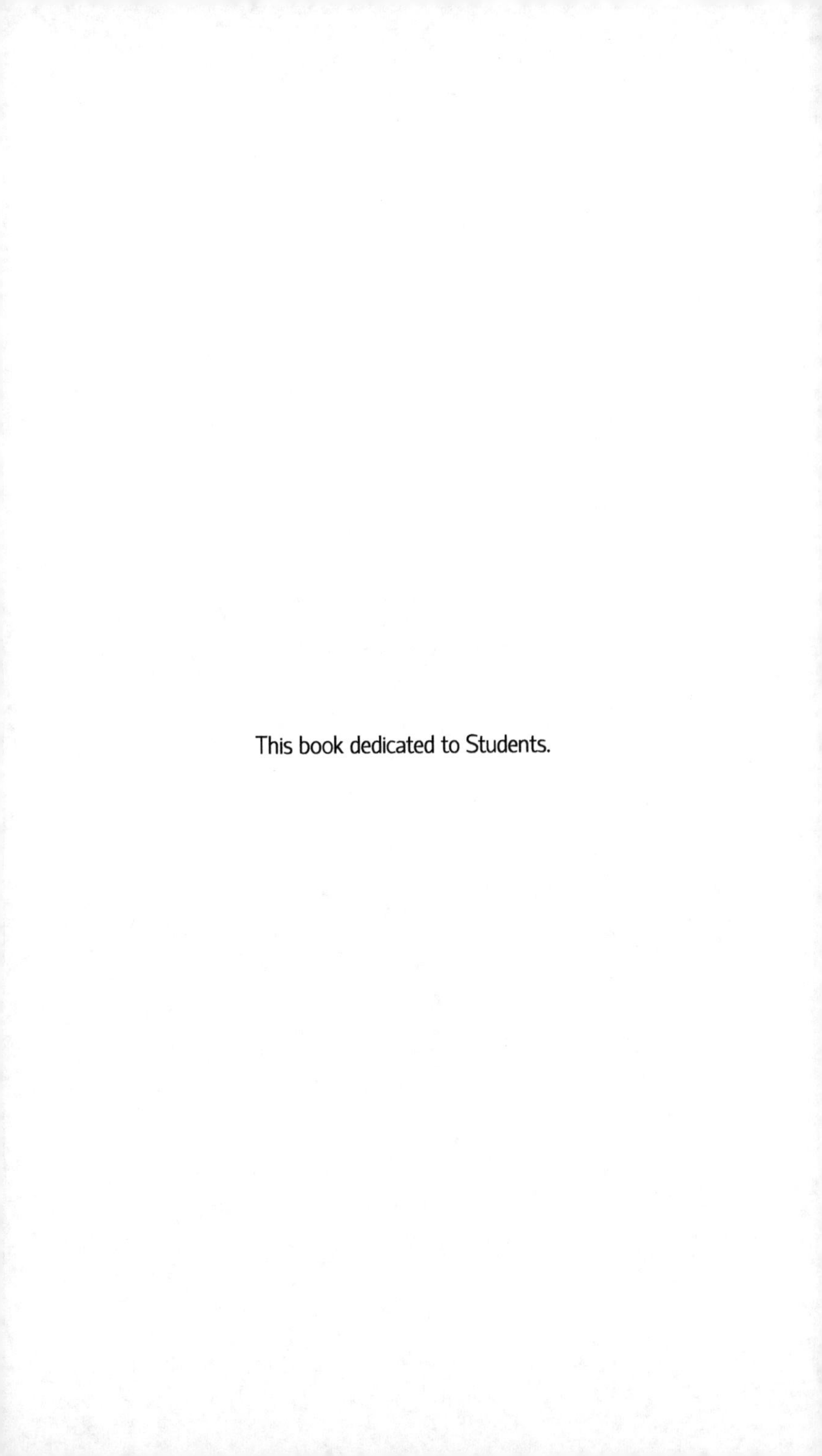

This book dedicated to Students.

Contents

Foreword

Cloud computing is information technology (IT) offered as a service. It eliminates the need for organizations to build and maintain expensive data centers. It enables organizations to stand up new systems quickly and easily. It provides elastic resources that allow applications to scale as needed in response to market demands. Its pay-as-you-go rental model allows organizations to defer costs. It increases business continuity by providing inexpensive disaster-recovery options. It reduces the need for organizations to maintain a large IT staff.

Preface

Cloud Computing Technique enables simplified functionality of infrastructure and platforms used in IT and IT-enabled industries, so that the end-users can avail what they want and pay only for the service they use.

Cloud Computing can be characterized as Internet-based computing in which many remote servers are networked to enable shared data-processing ventures, centralized knowledge storage, and access to services or resources online. The term 'Cloud Computing' is relatively new but unknowingly, we have been engaging the cloud, when Hotmail and other Web-based emails gained popularity.

Acknowledgements

We would like to express our gratitude to all the professors and researchers who contributed to this, our first, book and to all those who provided support, talked things over, or read, wrote, and offered comments.

Thanks also to the following reviewers who read the manuscript at different stages of its development, for their feedback and comments:

Prologue

Cloud computing is changing strategies and enabling innovation at every turn. Cloud is changing IT economics. Cloud is blurring the lines and breaking down traditional silos. Cloud is blending roles and redefining boundaries. Regardless of which industry we are in, or the position we hold, cloud computing is changing everything: how we work, how we play, and how we communicate.

CHAPTER ONE

INTRODUCTION TO SERVICE ORIENTED ARCHITECTURE

Advance Cloud Computing

Unit - 1

INTRODUCTION TO SERVICE ORIENTED ARCHITECTURE

Service-Oriented Architecture (SOA) is an architectural approach in which applications make use of services available in the network. In this architecture, services are provided to form applications, through a communication call over the internet.

- SOA allows users to combine a large number of facilities from existing services to form applications.
- SOA encompasses a set of design principles that structure system development and provide means for integrating components into a coherent and decentralized system.
- SOA based computing packages functionalities into a set of interoperable services, which can be integrated into different software systems belonging to separate

business domains.

There are two major roles within Service-oriented Architecture:

1. Service provider: The service provider is the mainta

   iner of the service and the organization that makes available one or more services for others to use. To advertise services, the provider can publish them in a registry, together with a service contract that specifies the nature of the service, how to use it, the requirements for the service, and the fees charged.

2. Service consumer: The service consumer can locate the service metadata in the registry and develop the required client components to bind and use the service.

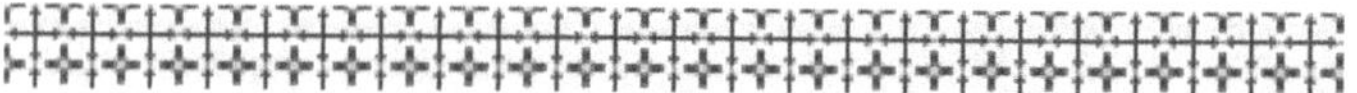

Figure 1.1 Service-oriented Architecture

Services might aggregate information and data retrieved from other services or create workflows of services to satisfy the request of a given service consumer. This practice is known as service orchestration another important interaction pattern is service choreography, which is the coordinated interaction of services without a single point of control.

Components of SOA

1. **Standardized service contract:** Specified through one or more service description documents.
2. **Loose coupling:** Services are designed as self-contained components, maintain relationships that minimize dependencies on other services.
3. **Abstraction:** A service is completely defined by service contracts and description documents. They hide their logic, which is encapsulated within their implementation.
4. **Reusability:** Designed as components, services can be reused more effectively, thus reducing development time and the associated costs.
5. **Autonomy:** Services have control over the logic they encapsulate and, from a service consumer point of view, there is no need to know about their implementation.
6. **Discoverability:** Services are defined by description documents that constitute supplemental metadata through which they can be effectively discovered. Service discovery provides an effective means for utilizing third-party resources.

WEB SERVICES

- A web service is any piece of software that makes itself available over the internet and uses a standardized XML messaging system. XML is used to encode all communications to a web service. For example, a client invokes a web service by sending an XML message, then waits for a corresponding XML response. As all communication is in XML, web services are not tied to any one operating system or programming language—Java can talk with Perl; Windows applications can talk with Unix applications.

- Web services are self-contained, modular, distributed, dynamic applications that can be described, published, located, or invoked over the network to create products, processes, and supply chains. These applications can be local, distributed, or web-based. Web services are built on top of open standards such as TCP/IP, HTTP, Java, HTML, and XML.

- Web services are XML-based information exchange systems that use the Internet for direct application-to-application interaction. These systems can include programs, objects, messages, or documents.

- A web service is a collection of open protocols and standards used for exchanging data between applications or systems. Software applications written in various programming languages and running on various platforms can use web services to exchange data over computer networks like the Internet in a manner similar to inter-process communication on a single computer. This interoperability (e.g., between Java and Python, or Windows and Linux applications) is due to the use of open standards.

Components of Web Services

The basic web services platform is XML + HTTP. All the standard web services work using the following components –

- SOAP (Simple Object Access Protocol)

- UDDI (Universal Description, Discovery and Integration)
- WSDL (Web Services Description Language)

BASIC WEB SERVICES ARCHITECTURE

Every framework needs some sort of architecture to make sure the entire framework works as desired, similarly, in web services. The Web Services Architecture consists of three distinct roles as given below:

1. **Provider** - The provider creates the web service and makes it available to client application who want to use it.
2. **Requestor** - A requestor is nothing but the client application that needs to contact a web service. The client application can be a .Net, Java, or any other language based application which looks for some sort of functionality via a web service.
3. **Broker** - The broker is nothing but the application which provides access to the UDDI. The UDDI, as discussed in the earlier topic enables the client application to locate the web service.

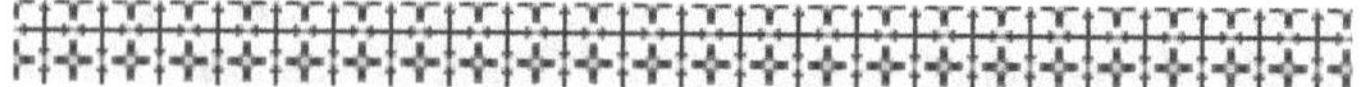

Figure 1.2 Basic Web Services Architecture

1. **Publish** - A provider informs the broker (service registry) about the existence of the web service by using the broker's publish interface to make the service accessible to clients
2. **Find** - The requestor consults the broker to locate a published web service
3. **Bind** - With the information it gained from the broker (service registry) about the web service, the requestor is able to bind, or invoke, the web service.

CHARACTERISTICS OF REST SERVICES

1. **Client-server based architecture:** Client/server architecture is a computing model in which the server

hosts, delivers and manages most of the resources and services to be consumed by the client. This type of architecture has one or more client computers connected to a central server over a network or internet connection. This system shares computing resources.

2. **Stateless:** This is the most important characteristic of a REST service. A REST HTTP request consists of all the data needed by the server to understand and give back the response. Once a request is served, the server doesn't remember if the request has arrived after a while. So the operation will be a stateless one.

3. **Cacheable:** Many developers think a technology stack is blocking their web application or API. But in reality, their architecture is the reason. The database can be a potential tuning piece in a web application. In order to scale an application well, we need to cache content and deliver it as a response. If the cache is not valid, it is our responsibility to bust it. REST services should be properly cached for scaling.

4. **Multiple layered system:** The REST API can be served from multiple servers. One server can request the other, and so forth. So when a request comes from the client, request and response can be passed between many servers to finally supply a response back to the client. This easily implementable multi-layered system is always a good strategy for keeping the web application loosely coupled.

5. **Representation of resources:** The REST API provides the uniform interface to talk to. It uses a Uniform Resource Identifier (URI) to map the resources (data). It also has the advantage of requesting a specific data format as the response. The Internet Media Type (MIME type) can tell the server that the requested

resource is of that particular type.

6. **Implementational freedom:** REST is just a mechanism to define your web services. It is an architectural style that can be implemented in multiple ways. Because of this flexibility, you can create REST services in the way you wish to. Until it follows the principles of REST, your server has the freedom to choose the platform or technology. Thoughtful caching is essential for the REST services to scale.

COMPONENTS

The basic components of cloud computing are divided into 3 (three) parts, namely clients, data-center, and distributed servers. The three basic components have specific goals and roles in running cloud computing operations. The concept of the three components can be described as follows:

1. **Clients** on cloud computing architecture are said to be the exact same things that are plain, old, everyday local area networks (LANs). They are, typically, the computers that just sit on your desk. But they might also be laptops, tablet computers, mobile phones, or PDAs - all big drivers for cloud computing because of their mobility. Clients are interacting with to manage their information on the cloud.

2. **Data-center** is collection of servers where the application to which you subscribe is housed. It could be a large room in the basement of your building full of servers on the other side of the world that you access via the Internet. A growing trend in the IT world is virtualizing servers. That is, software can be installed allowing multiple instances of virtual servers to be used.

In this way, you can have half a dozen virtual servers running on one physical server.

3. **Distributed Servers** is a server placement in a different location. But the servers don't have to be housed in the same location. Often, servers are in geographically disparate locations. But to you, the cloud subscribers, these servers act as if they're humming away right next to each other. Another component of cloud computing is Cloud Applications cloud computing in terms of software architecture. So that the user does not need to install and run applications using a computer. Cloud Platform is a service in the form of a computing platform that contains hardware infrastructure and software. Usually have certain business applications and use services PaaS as its business application infrastructure. Cloud Storage involves processes delivering data storage as a service. Cloud Infrastructure is the delivery of computing infrastructure as a service.

WEB SERVICES DESCRIPTION LANGUAGE

WSDL forms the basis for the original Web services specification. Figure 1.3 illustrates the use of WSDL. At the left is a service provider and at the right is a Service consumer. The steps involved in providing and consuming a service are as follows:

Figure 1.3 Web services basics

1. A service provider describes its service using WSDL. This definition is published to a registry of services. The registry uses UDDI.
2. A service consumer issues one or more queries to the registry to locate a service and determine how to communicate with that service.
3. Part of the WSDL provided by the service provider is passed to the service consumer. This tells the service consumer what the requests and responses are for the service provider.
4. The service consumer uses the WSDL to send a request to the service provider.
5. The service provider provides the expected response to the service consumer.

SOAP

All the messages shown in Figure 1.3 are sent using SOAP. (SOAP at one time stood for Simple Object Access Protocol; now the letters in the acronym have no particular meaning) SOAP provides the envelope for sending Web services messages. SOAP generally uses HTTP, but other means of connection may be used. HTTP is the familiar connection we all use for the Internet. Figure 1.4 provides more detail on the messages sent using Web services. At the left of the figure is a fragment of the WSDL sent to the registry. It shows a **CustomerInfoRequest** that requires the customer's account to object information. Also shown is the **CustomerInfoResponse** that provides a series of items on the customer including name, telephone, and address items. At the right of the figure is a

Figure 1.4 SOAP messaging with a directory

Fragment of the WSDL sent to the service consumer. This is the same fragment sent to the directory by the service provider. The service consumer uses this WSDL to create the service request shown above the arrow connecting the service consumer to the service provider.

Upon receiving the request, the service provider returns a message using the format described in the original WSDL. That message appears at the bottom of Figure 1.4.

UNIVERSAL DESCRIPTION, DISCOVERY AND INTEGRATION (UDDI)

The UDDI registry was intended to serve as a means of "discovering" Web services described using WSDL. The idea was that the UDDI registry could be searched in various ways to obtain contact information and the services available from various organizations. UDDI registries have not been widely implemented. The term registry is sometimes used interchangeably with the term service repository. Generally, repositories contain more information than a strict implementation of a UDDI registry. Today, instead of active discovery, repositories are used mainly at design time and to assist with governance.

UDDI is an XML-based standard for describing, publishing, and finding web services.

- UDDI stands for Universal Description, Discovery, and Integration.
- UDDI is a specification for a distributed registry of web services.
- UDDI is a platform-independent, open framework.
- UDDI can communicate via SOAP, CORBA, and Java RMI Protocol.
- UDDI uses Web Service Definition Language (WSDL) to describe interfaces to web services.
- UDDI is seen with SOAP and WSDL as one of the three foundation standards of web services.
- UDDI is an open industry initiative, enabling businesses to discover each other and define how they interact over the Internet.

UDDI has two sections

- A registry of all web service's metadata, including a pointer to the WSDL description of a service.
- A set of WSDL port type definitions for manipulating and searching that registry.

RESTFUL WEB SERVICES

RESTful web services are built to work best on the Web. Representational State Transfer (REST) is an architectural style that specifies constraints, such as the uniform interface, that if applied to a web service induce desirable properties, such as performance, scalability, and modifiability that enable services to work best on the Web. In the REST architectural style, data and functionality are considered resources and are accessed using Uniform Resource Identifiers (URIs), typically links on the Web. The resources are acted upon by using a set of simple, well-defined operations. The REST architectural style constrains an architecture to a client/server architecture and is designed to use a stateless communication protocol, typically HTTP. In the REST architecture style, clients and servers exchange representations of resources by using a standardized interface and protocol.

The following principles encourage RESTful applications to be simple, lightweight, and fast

- Resource identification through URI: A RESTful web service exposes a set of resources that identify the targets of the interaction with its clients. Resources are identified by URIs, which provide a global addressing space for resource and service discovery. See the @Path Annotation and URI Path Templates for more information.

- Uniform interface: Resources are manipulated using a fixed set of four create, read, update, delete operations: PUT, GET, POST, and DELETE. PUT creates a new resource, which can be then deleted by using DELETE. GET retrieves the current state of a resource in some representation. POST transfers a new state onto a resource. See Responding to HTTP Methods and Requests for more information.

- Self-descriptive messages: Resources are decoupled from their representation so that their content can be accessed in a variety of formats, such as HTML, XML, plain text, PDF, JPEG, JSON, and others. Metadata about the resource is available and used, for example, to control caching, detect transmission errors, negotiate the appropriate representation format, and perform authentication or access control. See Responding to HTTP Methods and Requests and Using Entity Providers to Map HTTP Response and Request Entity Bodies for more information.

- Stateful interactions through hyperlinks: Every interaction with a resource is stateless; that is, request messages are self-contained. Stateful interactions are based on the concept of explicit state transfer. Several techniques exist to exchange state, such as URI rewriting, cookies, and hidden form fields. State can be embedded in response messages to point to valid future states of the interaction. See Using Entity Providers to Map HTTP Response and Request Entity Bodies and "Building URIs" in the JAX-RS Overview document for more information.

SOFTWARE AS A SERVICE (SAAS)

Software as a Service provides you with a completed product that is run and managed by the service provider. In most cases, people referring to Software as a Service are referring to end-user applications. With a SaaS offering you do not have to think about how the service is maintained or how the underlying infrastructure is managed; you only need to think about how you will use that particular piece software. A common example of a SaaS application is web-based email where you can send and receive email without having to manage feature additions to the email product or maintaining the servers and operating systems that the email program is running on.

PLATFORM AS A SERVICE (PAAS)

Platforms as a service remove the need for organizations to manage the underlying infrastructure (usually hardware and operating systems) and allow you to focus on the deployment and management of your applications. This helps you be more efficient as you don't need to worry about resource procurement, capacity planning, software maintenance, patching, or any of the other undifferentiated heavy lifting involved in running your application.

PUBLIC, PRIVATE AND HYBRID CLOUDS

The concept of cloud computing has evolved from cluster, grid, and utility computing. Cluster and grid computing leverage the use of many computers in parallel to solve problems of any large numbers of services to end users. Cloud computing is a high throughput computing (HTC) paradigm whereby the infrastructure provides the services through a large data center or server farms. The cloud computing model enables users to share access to resources from anywhere at any time through their connected devices. In this scenario, the computations (programs) are sent to where the data is located, rather than copying the data to millions of desktops as in the traditional approach. Cloud computing avoids large data movement, resulting in much better network bandwidth utilization. Furthermore, machine virtualization has enhanced resource utilization, increased application flexibility, and reduced the total cost of using virtualized data center resources. The cloud offers significant benefit to IT companies by freeing them from the low-level task of setting up the hardware (servers) and managing the system software. Cloud computing applies a virtual platform with elastic resources put together by on demand provisioning of hardware, software, and data sets, dynamically. The main idea is to move desktop computing to a service-oriented platform using server clusters and huge databases at data centers. Cloud computing leverages its low cost and simplicity to both providers and users. According to Ian Foster, cloud computing intends to leverage multitasking to achieve higher throughput by serving many heterogeneous applications, large or small, simultaneously.

Public Clouds

A public cloud built over the Internet and accessed by any user who has paid for the service. Public clouds owned by service providers and accessible through a subscription the callout box in top of the architecture of a typical public cloud many public clouds are available, including Google App Engine (GAE), Amazon Web Services (AWS), Microsoft Azure, IBM Blue Cloud, and Force.com. The providers for mentioned clouds are commercial providers that offer a publicly accessible remote interface for creating and managing VM instances within their proprietary infrastructure. A public cloud delivers a selected set of business processes. The application and infrastructure services offered on a flexible price peruse basis.

Private Clouds

A private cloud built within the domain of an intranet owned by a single organization. Therefore, it is client owned and managed, and its access is limited to the owning clients and their partners. Its deployment not meant to sell capacity over the Internet through publicly accessible interfaces. Private clouds give local users a flexible and agile private infrastructure to run service workloads within their administrative domains. A private cloud is supposed to deliver more efficient and convenient cloud services. It may affect the cloud standardization, while retaining greater customization and organizational control.

Hybrid Clouds

A hybrid cloud is built with both public and private clouds Private clouds can also support a hybrid cloud model by supplementing local infrastructure with computing capacity from an external public cloud. For example, the Research Compute Cloud (RC2) is a private cloud, built by IBM, that interconnects the computing and IT resources at eight IBM Research Centers scattered throughout the United States, Europe, and Asia. A hybrid cloud provides access to clients, the partner network, and third parties. In summary, public clouds promote standardization, preserve capital investment, and offer application flexibility. Private clouds attempt to achieve customization and offer higher efficiency, resiliency, security, and privacy. Hybrid clouds operate in the middle, with many compromises in terms of resource sharing.

ADMINISTERING CLOUD COMPUTING SERVICES

When managing cloud computing services, a company has to ask itself many questions about the various services' effectiveness. The administrators must know if the performance is at the right level, and they must be able to tell if data that has been deleted is really gone.

Solving these problems isn't easy. Investigating the reliability and viability of a cloud provider is one of the most complex areas faced when managing the cloud. The advent of cloud computing will be accompanied by disappointed customers and lawsuits for sure — some as a consequence of unrealistic expectations and some as a consequence of poor service.

Administering features of cloud

Traditional network management system offers the following fundamental features. These are:

- Resource administration
- Resource Configuration
- Security Enforcement
- Operations monitoring
- Provisioning of resources
- Management of policies
- Performance maintenance
- Performance optimizing

MONITORING CLOUD COMPUTING SERVICES

Cloud monitoring is the process of evaluating, monitoring, and managing cloud-based services, applications, and infrastructure. Companies utilize various application monitoring tools to monitor cloud-based applications. Here's a look at how it works and best practices for success.

How It Works

The term cloud refers to a set of web-hosted applications that store and allow access to data over the Internet instead of on a computer's hard drive.

- For consumers, simply using the internet to view web pages, access email accounts on services such as Gmail, and store files in Dropbox are examples of cloud computing for consumers.
- Businesses use it in many of the same ways. They also may use Software as a Service (SaaS) options to subscribe to business applications or rent server space to host proprietary applications to provide services to consumers.

Cloud monitoring works through a set of tools that supervise the servers, resources, and applications running the applications. These tools generally come from two sources:

1. **In-house tools from the cloud provider** - This is a simple option because the tools are part of the service. There is no installation, and integration is seamless.
2. **Tools from independent SaaS provider** - Although the SaaS provider may be different from the cloud service provider, that doesn't mean the two services don't work seamlessly. These providers also have expertise in managing performance and costs.

Cloud monitoring tools look for problems that can prevent or restrict businesses from delivering service to their customers. Generally, these tools offer data on performance, security, and customer behavior:

- Cybersecurity is a necessary part of <u>keeping networks safe</u> from cyber-attacks. IT teams can use it to detect breaches and vulnerabilities early and secure the network before the damage gets out of hand.
- By testing at regular intervals, organizations can detect errors quickly and rectify them in order to mitigate any damage to performance and functionality, which improves the customer experience and, as a result, can boost sales and enhance customer retention.
- Speed — like functionality and user experience — is a primary driver of customer satisfaction. Speed metrics can be monitored and generate data that helps organizations optimize websites and applications.

Types of cloud services to monitor

There are multiple types of cloud services to monitor. Cloud monitoring is not just about monitoring servers hosted on AWS or Azure. For enterprises, they also put a lot of importance into monitoring cloud-based services that they consume.

- **SaaS** – Services like Office 365, Salesforce and others
- **PaaS** – Developer friendly services like SQL databases, caching, storage and more
- **IaaS** – Servers hosted by cloud providers like Azure, AWS, Digital Ocean, and others
- **FaaS** – New server less applications like AWS Lambda and Azure Functions
- **Application Hosting** – Services like Azure App Services, Heroku, etc.

Benefits of Cloud Monitoring

- They already have infrastructure and configurations in place. Installation is quick and easy.
- Dedicated tools are maintained by the host. That includes hardware.
- These solutions are built for organizations of various sizes. So if cloud activity increases, the right monitoring tool can scale seamlessly.
- Subscription-based solutions can keep costs low. They do not require startup or infrastructure expenditures, and maintenance costs are spread among multiple users.
- Because the resources are not part of the organization's servers and workstations, they don't suffer interruptions when local problems disrupt the organization.
- Many tools can be used on multiple types of devices — desktop computers, tablets, and phones. This allows organizations to monitor apps and services from any location with Internet access.

BENEFITS AND LIMITATIONS
Benefits -

- *Data security*-One of the major concerns of every business, regardless of size and industry, is the security of its data as data breaches and other cybercrimes can devastate a company's revenue, customer loyalty and brand positioning. Cloud Computing offers many advanced security features that guarantee that data is securely stored and handled.

Cloud storage providers implement protections for their platforms and the data that they process, such as authentication, access control, and encryption.

- *Scalability* - If a company is anticipating a huge upswing in computing need, cloud computing can manage. Instead of buying and configuring new storage, cloud computing provides additional storage from third party.
- *Mobility* -Cloud computing allows mobile access to corporate data via smartphones and devices, which is a great way to ensure that no one is ever left out of the loop.

Staff with busy schedules, or who live a long way away from the corporate office, can use this feature to keep instantly up-to-date with clients and co-workers. Resources in the cloud can easily be made available for operations such as storing, retrieval, recovery, or processing with just a couple of clicks.

- *Control* - It is vital for any company to have control over sensitive data. You never know what can happen if a document gets into the wrong hands, even if it's just the hands of an untrained employee. Cloud gives you complete visibility and control over your data. The level of access to particular data can be easily decided.

Limitations -

- *Control of data security* - In a public cloud, an individual does not have control over the security of his/her data, which makes the client's data susceptible to hacking. Even though highest security measures are taken into effect, data security is limited to an extent after which data might be lost or leaked.

- **Network connection** - In order for the cloud to perform its basic functions, a reliable internet connection is needed. If there are problems of network connectivity, accessing the cloud will be a problem.
- **Peripheral devices** - Most commonly used peripheral devices such as printers and scanners might not be compatible with the cloud and thus interrupt normal functioning. They usually require a local software to be installed in order for proper compatibility. On the other hand, network peripherals have lesser problems.
- **Additional Costs** - Although Cloud computing is economical/cost-effective, there might be some hidden or additional costs such as charging a client for data transfer or other tasks which are not common.

STUDY OF HYPERVISOR

A hypervisor, also known as a virtual machine monitor or VMM, is software that creates and runs virtual machines (VMs). A hypervisor allows one host computer to support multiple guest VMs by virtually sharing its resources, such as memory and processing.

Hypervisors make it possible to use more of a system's available resources and provide greater IT mobility since the guest VMs are independent of the host hardware. This means they can be easily moved between different servers. Because multiple virtual machines can run off of one physical server with a hypervisor, a hypervisor reduces Space, Energy and .Maintenance requirements

The hypervisor has emerged as an invaluable tool for running virtual machines and driving innovation in a cloud environment. Since a hypervisor is a software layer that enables one host computer to simultaneously support multiple VMs, hypervisors are a key element of the technology that makes cloud computing possible. Hypervisors make cloud-based applications available to users across a virtual environment while still enabling IT to maintain control over a cloud environment's infrastructure, applications and sensitive data.

Digital transformation and rising customer expectations are driving greater reliance on innovative applications. In response, many enterprises are migrating their virtual machines to the cloud. However, having to rewrite every existing application for the cloud can consume precious IT resources and lead to infrastructure silos. Fortunately, as an integral part of a virtualization platform, a hypervisor can help migrate applications to the cloud quickly. As a result, enterprises can reap the cloud's many benefits, including reduced hardware expenditures, increased accessibility and greater scalability, for a faster return on investment.

Benefits of hypervisors

There are several benefits to using a hypervisor that hosts multiple virtual machines:

1. Speed: Hypervisors allow virtual machines to be created instantly, unlike bare-metal servers. This makes it easier to provision resources as needed for dynamic workloads.

2. Efficiency: Hypervisors that run several virtual machines on one physical machine's resources also allow for more efficient utilization of one physical server. It is more cost- and energy-efficient to run several virtual machines on one physical machine than to run multiple underutilized physical machines for the same task.

3. Flexibility: Bare-metal hypervisors allow operating systems and their associated applications to run on a variety of hardware types because the hypervisor separates the OS from the underlying hardware, so the software no longer relies on specific hardware devices or drivers.

4. Portability: Hypervisors allow multiple operating systems to reside on the same physical server (host machine). Because the virtual machines that the hypervisor runs are independent from the physical machine, they are portable. IT teams can shift workloads and allocate networking, memory, storage and processing resources across multiple servers as needed, moving from machine to machine or platform to platform. When an application needs more processing power, the virtualization software allows it to seamlessly access additional machines.

CHAPTER TWO

UTILITY COMPUTING

Advance Cloud Computing

Unit-2

UTILITY COMPUTING

Utility computing is a service provisioning model in which a service provider makes computing resources and infrastructure management available to the customer as needed, and charges them for specific usage rather than a flat rate. Like other types of on-demand computing (such as grid computing), the utility model seeks to maximize the efficient use of resources and/or minimize associated costs.

The word utility is used to make an analogy to other services, such as electrical power, that seek to meet fluctuating customer needs, and charge for the resources based on usage rather than on a flat-rate basis. This approach, sometimes known as pay-per-use or metered services is becoming increasingly common in enterprise computing and is sometimes used for the consumer market as well, for Internet service, Web site access, file sharing, and other applications.

Another version of utility computing is carried out within an enterprise. In a shared pool utility model, an enterprise centralizes its computing resources to serve a larger number of users without unnecessary redundancy.

Properties of utility computing

Following are characteristics of utility computing.

1. Scalability: The utility computing must be ensured that under all conditions sufficient IT resources are available. Increasing the demand for a service may, its quality (e.g., response time) does not suffer.

2. Demand pricing: So far, companies have to buy his own hardware and software when they need computing power. This IT infrastructure must be paid in advance of the rule, regardless of the intensity with which the company uses them later. Technology vendors to achieve this link, for example, the fact that the lease rate for their servers depends on how many CPUs has enabled the customer. If it can be measured in a company as much computing power to claim the individual sections in fact, may be the IT costs in internal cost directly attributable to the individual departments. Other forms of connection with the use of IT costs are possible.

3. Standardized Utility Computing Services: The utility computing service provider offers its customers a catalogue of standardized services. These may have different service level agreements (Agreement on the quality and the price of an IT) services. The customer has no influence on the underlying technologies such as the server platform.

4. Utility Computing and Virtualization: To share the web and other resources in the shared pool of machines can be used virtualization technologies. This will divide the network into logical resource instead of the physical resources available. An application is assigned no

specific pre-determined servers or storage of any but a free server runtime or memory from the pool.

5. Automation: Repetitive management tasks such as setting up a new server or the installation of updates can be automated. Moreover, automatically allocate resources to services and the management of IT services to be optimized, with service level agreements and operating costs of IT resources must be considered.

Advantages of Utility Computing

Utility computing reduces the cost of IT, given that existing resources can be used more effectively. Moreover, the costs are transparent and the various departments of a company can be directly assigned. In the cs departments will be fewer people needed for operational activities.

The companies achieve greater flexibility, because their IT resources more quickly and easily adapt to fluctuating demand. Overall, it is easier to manage the entire IT structure, as there will no longer be made for each application, which is a benefit for specific IT infrastructure.

ELASTIC COMPUTING

Elastic computing is the ability to quickly expand or decrease computer processing, memory and storage resources to meet changing demands without worrying about capacity planning and engineering for peak usage.

Elastic computing is a concept in cloud computing in which computing resources can be scaled up and down easily by the cloud service provider. Elastic computing is the ability of a cloud service provider to provision flexible computing power when and wherever required. The elasticity of these resources can be in terms of processing power, storage, bandwidth, etc.

Cloud computing is about provisioning on-demand computing resources with the simplicity of a mouse click. The amount of resources which can be sourced through cloud computing incorporates almost all the facets of computing from raw processing power to massive storage space.

Besides providing these services on demand basis, the resources are elastic in nature, i.e. they can be easily scaled depending upon the underlying resource requirements on run time without even disrupting the operations and this ability is known as elastic computing. On a small scale this is done manually, but for larger installations, the scaling is automatic. For example, a larger provider of online video could setup a system so that the number of web-servers online scaled during peak viewing hours.

Benefits of Elastic Cloud Computing

Elastic Cloud Computing has numerous advantages. Some of them are as follow:-

1. **Cost Efficiency:** – Cloud is available at much cheaper rates than traditional approaches and can significantly lower the overall IT expenses. By using cloud solution companies can save licensing fees as well as eliminate overhead charges such as the cost of data storage, software updates, management etc.

2. **Convenience and continuous availability:** – Cloud makes easier access of shared documents and files with view and modifies choice. Public clouds also offer services that are available wherever the end user might be located. Moreover it guaranteed continuous availability of resources and In case of system failure; alternative instances are automatically spawned on other machines.

3. **Backup and Recovery:** – The process of backing up and recovering data is easy as information is residing on cloud simplified and not on a physical device. The various cloud providers offer reliable and flexible backup/recovery solutions.

4. **Cloud is environmentally friendly:**-The cloud is more efficient than the typical IT infrastructure and it takes fewer resources to compute, thus saving energy.

5. **Scalability and Performance:** – Scalability is a built-in feature for cloud deployments. Cloud instances are deployed automatically only when needed and as a result enhance performance with excellent speed of computations.

6. **Increased Storage Capacity:**-The cloud can accommodate and store much more data compared to a personal computer and in a way offers almost unlimited storage capacity.

Disadvantages/Cons of Elastic Cloud Computing:-

1. **Security and Privacy in the Cloud:** – Security is the biggest concern in cloud computing. Companies essentially hide their private data and information over cloud as remote based cloud infrastructure is used, it is then up to the cloud service provider to manage, protect and retain data confidential.

2. **Limited Control:** – Since the applications and services are running remotely companies, users and third party virtual environments have limited control over the function and execution of the hardware and software.

3. **Dependency and vendor lock-in:** – One of the major drawbacks of cloud computing is the implicit dependency on the provider. It is also called "vendor

lock-in". As it becomes difficult to migrated vast data from old provider to new. So, it is advisable to select vendor very carefully.

4. **Increased Vulnerability**: – Cloud based solutions are exposed on the public internet therefore is more vulnerable target for malicious users and hackers. As we know nothing is completely secure over Internet even the biggest organizations also suffer from serious attacks and security breaches.

AJAX: ASYNCHRONOUS 'RICH' INTERFACES

AJAX stands for Asynchronous JavaScript and XML. AJAX is a new technique for creating better, faster, and more interactive web applications with the help of XML, HTML, CSS, and Java Script.

- Ajax uses XHTML for content, CSS for presentation, along with Document Object Model and JavaScript for dynamic content display.
- Conventional web applications transmit information to and from the sever using synchronous requests. It means you fill out a form, hit submit, and get directed to a new page with new information from the server.
- With AJAX, when you hit submit, JavaScript will make a request to the server, interpret the results, and update the current screen. In the purest sense, the user would never know that anything was even transmitted to the server.
- XML is commonly used as the format for receiving server data, although any format, including plain text, can be used.
- AJAX is a web browser technology independent of web server software.

- A user can continue to use the application while the client program requests information from the server in the background.
- Intuitive and natural user interaction. Clicking is not required; mouse movement is a sufficient event trigger.
- Data-driven as opposed to page-driven.

Rich Internet Application Technology

AJAX is the most viable Rich Internet Application (RIA) technology so far. It is getting tremendous industry momentum and several tool kit and frameworks are emerging. But at the same time, AJAX has browser incompatibility and it is supported by JavaScript, which is hard to maintain and debug.

AJAX is based on Open Standards

AJAX is based on the following open standards –

- Browser-based presentation using HTML and Cascading Style Sheets (CSS).
- Data is stored in XML format and fetched from the server.
- Behind-the-scenes data fetches using XMLHttpRequest objects in the browser.
- JavaScript to make everything happen.

Important Features of Ajax

- User Friendly.
- It make web page faster.
- Independent of server technology.
- Increase the Performance of web page.
- Support for Live data binding.
- Support for the Data View control.

- No need to pushing on a submit button and reloading the complete website.
- No need to reload the whole page only some part of page is reloaded which is required to reload.
- Not require to completely reload page due to this server use less bandwidth.

MASHUPS: USER INTERFACE

The term 'mash-up' refers to websites that weave data from different sources into new Web services. The key to a successful Web service is to gather and use large datasets and harness the scale of the Internet through what is known as network effects.

The main characteristics of the mashup are combination, visualization, and aggregation. It is important to make existing data more useful, moreover for personal and professional use. To be able to permanently access the data of other services, mashups are generally client applications or hosted online.

In the past years, more and more Web applications have published APIs that enable software developers to easily integrate data and functions instead of building them by themselves. Mashups can be considered to have an active role in the evolution of social software and Web 2.0. Mashup composition tools are usually simple enough to be used by end-users. They generally do not require programming skills and rather support visual wiring of GUI widgets, services and components together. Therefore, these tools contribute to a new vision of the Web, where users are able to contribute.

Figure 2.1 Mashups

Characteristics of mashups

We could infer the following outstanding characteristics of mashups, based on the concepts mentioned above:

- A mashup is focused on adding value, putting a tremendous amount of ready information at the fingertips of the final user.
- Information + User experience should be efficiently combined, using technologies such as RIAs.
- It prioritizes the information in the order in which is most likely to be useful. You have to know who you are talking to, what products they have registered, what the top service items are for those products, and then start trying to answer questions that they may have such as

where the local service centres' are for the customer's location.

- Developing a mashup must be measured in hours or eays.
- Generally, it is read-only.
- Mashups are agile views into the data that they present. They are not an all-powerful editing surface capable of editing any and all data thrown at them. If someone wants to edit that data, they should go back to the application that created the data to do the editing. A timestamp may be important for improving the clarity and usefulness of the mashed data.

Types of the Mashup

There are many types of mashup, such as business mashups, consumer mashups, and data mashups. The most common type of mashup is the consumer mashup, aimed at the general public.

- Business (or enterprise) mashups define applications that combine their own resources, application and data, with other external Web services. They focus data into a single presentation and allow for collaborative action among businesses and developers. This works well for an agile development project, which requires collaboration between the developers and customer (or customer proxy, typically a product manager) for defining and implementing the business requirements. Enterprise mashups are secure, visually rich Web applications that expose actionable information from diverse internal and external information sources.
- Consumer mashups combine data from multiple public sources in the browser and organize it through a simple

browser user interface.

- Data mashups, opposite to the consumer mashups, combine similar types of media and information from multiple sources into a single representation. The combination of all these resources creates a new and distinct Web service that was not originally provided by either source.

VIRTUALIZATION TECHNOLOGY: VIRTUALIZATION APPLICATIONS IN ENTERPRISES

Virtualization means that the users (programs or people) only see an abstraction of a computer resource. Virtualization can be done in software, or with hardware. Virtualization is the creation of virtual servers, infrastructures, devices and computing resources. Virtualization changes the hardware-software relations and is one of the foundational elements of cloud computing technology that helps utilize the capabilities of cloud computing to the full. Virtualization techniques allow companies to turn their networks, storage, servers, data, desktops and applications virtual.

Figure 2.2 virtualization work in cloud computing

Types of Virtualization in Cloud Computing

1. Operating System Virtualization

In operating system virtualization in Cloud Computing, the virtual machine software installs in the operating system of the host rather than directly on the hardware system. The most important use of operating system virtualization is for testing the application on different platforms or operating system. Here, the software is present in the hardware, which allows different applications to run.

1. Hardware Virtualization

<u>Hardware virtualization</u> in Cloud Computing, used in server platform as it is flexible to use Virtual Machine rather than physical machines. In hardware virtualizations, virtual machine software installs in the hardware system and then it is known as hardware virtualization. It consists of a hypervisor which use to control and monitor the process, memory, and other hardware resources. After the completion of hardware virtualization process, the user can install the different operating system in it and with this platform different application can use.

3. Server Virtualization

In <u>server virtualization</u> in Cloud Computing, the software directly installs on the server system and use for a single physical server can divide into many servers on the demand basis and balance the load. It can be also stated that the server virtualization is masking of the server resources which consists of number and identity. With the help of software, the server administrator divides one physical server into multiple servers.

4. Storage Virtualization

In <u>storage virtualization</u> in Cloud Computing, a grouping is done of physical storage which is from multiple network storage devices this is done so it looks like a single storage device. It can implement with the help of software applications and storage virtualization is done for the backup and recovery process. It is a sharing of the physical storage from multiple storage devices.

5. Network Virtualization

With network virtualization, you can create multiple individual networks from one physical local area network (LAN). In terms of the cloud, you're looking at trying to create an 'online' network <u>without</u> connecting to the public internet (i.e., virtual private cloud).

6. Application Virtualization

With application virtualization, you're running an application on a computer, but without relying on the computer's hardware or software.

Returning to the iPad example; you may not be able to run full Photoshop on the iPad directly. But you can get the iPad to speak to a Windows-based server running full Photoshop and, in turn, use your iPad to access Photoshop.

An upcoming evolution of this is <u>cloud-based console gaming</u>. So again, you can use an iPad, iPhone, etc., to play full console games by relying on a server with enough power to run them.

7. Scalability Is Key

One of the great advantages of the virtualization model, and indeed of cloud computing in general, is scalability. Migrating to the cloud allows your applications and storage to scale with your needs, and you don't even have to lift a finger to do it.

To take full advantage of this scalability factor, you need to migrate everything that matters to the cloud, a painstaking process that's best left to the experts – like us. At Network Coverage, we have years of experience in providing cloud and IT services to enterprise customers. <u>Contact us now for a free consultation</u>, and we can help you virtualizes your servers or fully enter the cloud.

Benefits of Virtualization

1. **Security:** During the process of virtualization security is one of the important concerns. The security can be provided with the help of firewalls, which will help to prevent unauthorized access and will keep the data confidential. Moreover, with the help of firewall and security, the data can protect from harmful viruses malware and other cyber threats. Encryption process also takes place with protocols which will protect the data from other threads. So, the customer can virtualizes all the data store and can create a backup on a server in which the data can store.

2. **Flexible operations:** With the help of a virtual network, the work of it professional is becoming more efficient and agile. The network switch implement today is very easy to use, flexible and saves time. With the help of virtualization in Cloud Computing, technical problems can solve in physical systems. It eliminates the problem of recovering the data from crashed or corrupted devices and hence saves time.

3. **Economical:** Virtualization in Cloud Computing, save the cost for a physical system such as hardware and servers. It stores all the data in the virtual server, which are quite economical. It reduces the wastage, decreases the electricity bills along with the maintenance cost. Due to this, the business can run multiple operating system and apps in a particular server.

4. **Eliminates the risk of system failure:** While performing some task there are chances that the system

might crash down at the wrong time. This failure can cause damage to the company but the virtualizations help you to perform the same task in multiple devices at the same time. The data can store in the cloud it can retrieve anytime and with the help of any device. Moreover, there is two working server side by side which makes the data accessible every time. Even if a server crashes with the help of the second server the customer can access the data.

5. **Flexible transfer of data:** The data can transfer to the virtual server and retrieve anytime. The customers or cloud provider don't have to waste time finding out hard drives to find data. With the help of virtualization, it will very easy to locate the required data and transfer them to the allotted authorities. This transfer of data has no limit and can transfer to a long distance with the minimum charge possible. Additional storage can also provide and the cost will be as low as possible.

PITFALLS OF VIRTUALIZATION MULTITENANT SOFTWARE: MULTI-ENTITY SUPPORT

Virtualization provides amazing value at the infrastructure level, particularly in terms of driving down operating costs through utilization increases, automation, and infrastructure flexibility.

The virtualization should focus on its strengths, and outside of rare instances, avoid venturing up stack to solve what are fundamentally software architecture problems (e.g. multi-tenancy, scale-out, etc.) It's true that moving to a multi-tenant architecture would require significant effort, but a lot has changed in the market. Technologies exist that can blunt the cost of adopting true multi-tenancy and SaaS architecture models to near trivial levels, negating much of the argument that it's difficult and costly (which is only the case if done ground up)

The "does virtualization obviate the need for multi-tenancy question" is odd if we think of it in different terms. For example, it's the same as asking **"does a faster processor solve the problem of slow data sorting?"** or **"does more memory on my computer make my memory hungry application faster?"** Clearly, a faster processor will make data sorting faster, but is a Band-Aid while a solution would be using/creating more efficient sorting algorithms. In the same vein, more RAM on your computer might make your memory intensive application run faster since your PC doesn't have to page to disk, but the solution might be to write a leaner application (which gives you an unbounded fix as opposed to the inherent limitations associated with adding more RAM or a faster processor).

MULTISCHEMA APPROACH

Each tenant's data is kept in a distinct database schema on a single database instance. There are 2 different ways to define JDBC Connections here:

- Connections could point specifically to each schema, as we saw with the Separate database approach. This is an option provided that the driver supports naming the default schema in the connection URL or if the pooling mechanism supports naming a schema to use for its Connections. Using this approach, we would have a distinct JDBC Connection pool per-tenant where the pool to use would be selected based on the "tenant identifier" associated with the currently logged in user.
- Connections could point to the database itself (using some default schema) but the Connections would be altered using the SQL SET SCHEMA (or similar)

command. Using this approach, we would have a single JDBC Connection pool for use to service all tenants, but before using the Connection it would be altered to reference the schema named by the "tenant identifier" associated with the currently logged in user.

Figure 2.3 Multischema Approach

Limitations

Currently, following known limitations apply to the multi-schema multi-tenancy (MS-MT) feature:

- As with regular multi-tenancy, it is not possible to configure the out of the box LDAP synchronization to synchronize users to different tenants.
- The tenant can only be configured through the REST API, not via the "identity management" app.
- Users need to be created by a user that is a "Tenant Administrator", not a "Tenant Manager".
- Updating a tenant configuration (more specifically: switching the data source) cannot be done dynamically, a restart of all nodes is required for it to be picked up.

- A user id needs to be unique across all tenants (cft. an email). This is because a mapping {user id, tenant id} will be stored in the primary database to determine the correct tenant data source.

MULTI-TENANCY USING CLOUD DATA STORES

A multi-tenant cloud is a cloud computing architecture that allows customers to share computing resources in a public or private cloud. Each tenant's data is isolated and remains invisible to other tenants.

In a multi-tenant cloud system, users have individualized space for storing their projects and data. Each section of a cloud network with multi-tenant architecture includes complex permissions with the intention of allowing each user access to only their stored information along with security from other cloud tenants. Within the cloud infrastructure, each tenant's data is inaccessible to all other tenants, and can only be reached with the cloud provider's permissions.

In a private cloud, the customers, or tenants, may be different individuals or groups within a single company, while in a public cloud; entirely different organizations may safely share their server space. Most public cloud providers use the multi-tenancy model. It allows them to run servers with single instances, which is less expensive and helps to streamline updates.

Figure 2.4 Multi-tenant cloud work

Multi-tenant cloud vs single-tenant cloud

In a single-tenant cloud, only one customer is hosted on a server and is granted access to it. Due to multi-tenancy architectures hosting multiples customers on the same servers, it is important to fully understand the security and performance the provider is offering. Single-tenant clouds give customers more control over the management of data, storage, security and performance.

Figure 2.5 Multi-tenant VS. Single -tenant

Benefits of multi-tenant cloud

Multi-tenant cloud networks provide increased storage and improved access compared to single-tenancy clouds that include limited access and security parameters. Multi-tenancy in cloud computing makes a greater pool of resources available to a larger group of people without sacrificing privacy and security or slowing down applications. The virtualization of storage locations in cloud computing allows for flexibility and ease of access from almost any device or location.

Advantages of Multi-tenancy:

- Multi-tenancy reduces cost by sharing same power resources and software across its clients. The software requires licenses and support, and the cost for this will increase if you need to buy them for each customer, as in the case of single-tenancy. Shared infrastructure will automatically lead to lower costs.

- In a multi-tenant application, you'll only have to monitor and provide administration for a single platform, unlike single-tenant applications where you have to manage different sets for each client. This way a multi-tenant SaaS provider can deliver more efficient and effective support, including problem resolution and troubleshooting.

- A multi-tenant architecture will make it easy for you to increase your capacity when more strength & power is required. The total capacity of the entire system increases and becomes more scalable when you bring in new hardware to the platform, not for merely a single client but all associated clients. Adding features for a single client makes it available to other clients.

- Upgrading the software version or system resources for multi-tenant applications are easy since there is a single, centralized place for up gradation, installation and more.

Disadvantages of Multi-tenancy:

- A multi-tenant app has lesser flexibility than a single-tenant app to set low-level configurations. This might not be a problem for you, but if your application requires a lot of customization for each new tenant, then a multi-tenant app might not be the best solution.

- A multi-tenant app is more complex than an equivalent single-tenant app, whose configuration can remain essentially static. In a single-tenant application, you don't require any code to detect which tenant a web request is intended for or to protect your clients from the leakage of data between tenants. The log formats are simpler since logs are segregated with a separate instance of the application for each client.

- Since a multi-tenant application is backed by a single database, running on a single server, it has lesser areas prone to failure, but those failure points can prove a lot more disastrous. All tenants experience loss of service when the database for a multitenant app is unavailable, unlike when a single-tenant application instance breaks. It brings down a single tenant. Other instances continue unaffected.

Example of multi-tenancy

Multi-tenant clouds can be compared to the structure of an apartment building. Each resident has access to their own apartment within the agreement of the entire building and only authorized individuals can enter the specific units. However, the entire building shares resources such as water, electricity and common areas.

This is similar to a multi-tenant cloud in that the provider sets overarching quotas, rules and performance expectations for customers but each individual customer has private access to their information.

CHAPTER THREE

DATA IN THE CLOUD: RELATIONAL DATABASES

Advance Cloud Computing

Unit-3

DATA IN THE CLOUD: RELATIONAL DATABASES

A relational database is a collection of data items with pre-defined relationships between them. These items are organized as a set of tables with columns and rows. Tables are used to hold information about the objects to be represented in the database. Each column in a table holds a certain kind of data and a field stores the actual value of an attribute.

The rows in the table represent a collection of related values of one object or entity. Each row in a table could be marked with a unique identifier called a primary key, and rows among multiple tables can be made related using foreign keys.

Important Aspects of Relational Databases:

SQL (Structured Query Language):

- SQL or Structured Query Language is the primary interface used to communicate with Relational Databases. SQL became a standard of the American National Standards Institute (ANSI) in 1986.

- The standard ANSI SQL is supported by all popular relational database engines, and some of these engines also have an extension to ANSI SQL to support functionality that is specific to that engine.
- SQL is used to add, update or delete rows of data, retrieving subsets of data for transaction processing and analytics applications, and to manage all aspects of the database.

Data Integrity:

- Data integrity is the overall completeness, accuracy, and consistency of data. Relational databases use a set of constraints to enforce data integrity in the database.
- These include primary Keys, Foreign Keys, 'Not NULL' constraint, 'Unique' constraint, 'Default' constraint, and 'Check' constraints. These integrity constraints help enforce business rules on data in the tables to ensure the accuracy and reliability of the data.

Transactions:

- A database transaction is one or more SQL statements that are executed as a sequence of operations that form a single logical unit of work.
- Transactions provide an "all-or-nothing" proposition, meaning that the entire transaction must complete as a single unit and be written to the database or none of the individual components of the transaction should go through.
- In the relation database terminology, a transaction results in a COMMIT or a ROLLBACK. Each transaction is treated coherently and reliably independent of other transactions.

ACID Compliance:

- Atomicity requires that either transaction be successfully executed or if a part of the transaction fails, then the entire transaction be invalidated.
- Consistency mandates the data written to the database as part of the transaction must adhere to all defined rules, and restrictions including constraints, cascades, and triggers.

- Isolation is critical to achieving concurrency control and makes sure each transaction is independent unto itself.

- Durability requires that all changes made to the database be permanent once a transaction is successfully completed.

CLOUD FILE SYSTEMS: GFS AND HDFS

Google file system (GFS):

- The Google File System (GFS) is a scalable distributed file system for large distributed data-intensive applications. It provides fault tolerance while running on inexpensive commodity hardware and it delivers high aggregate performance to a large number of clients.
- GFS provides a familiar file system interface, though it does not implement a standard API such as POSIX.
- Files are organized hierarchically in directories and identified by path-names. GFS supports the usual operations such as create, delete, open, close, read, and write files.
- GFS has snapshot and record appends operations. Snapshot creates a copy of a file or a directory tree at a low cost.

The architecture of GFS:

Figure 3.1 Google file system architecture

- A GFS cluster consists of a single master and multiple chunk servers and is accessed by multiple clients.
- Each of these is typically a commodity Linux machine running a user-level server process.
- Files are divided into fixed-size chunks. Each chunk is identified by a fixed and globally unique 64-bit chunk handle assigned by the master at the time of chunk creation. Chunk servers store chunks on local disks as Linux files.
- The master maintains the metadata, which includes the namespace, access control information, the mapping from files to chunks, and the current locations of chunks.
- GFS client code linked into each application to implement the file system API and communicates with the master & chunk servers to read or write data on behalf of the application.
- Clients interact with the master for metadata operations, but all data-bearing communication goes directly to the chunk servers.

Hadoop distributed file system (HDFS):

Hadoop File System was developed using distributed file system design. It runs on commodity hardware. HDFS holds a very large amount of data and provides easier access. To store such huge data, the files are stored across multiple machines. These files are stored redundantly to rescue the system from possible data losses in case of failure.

The architecture of HDFS:

Figure 3.2 HDFS Architecture

HDFS follows the master-slave architecture and it has the following elements.

NameNode:

The NameNode is the commodity hardware that contains the GNU/Linux operating system and the NameNode software. It is software that can be run on commodity hardware. The system having the NameNode acts as the master server and it does the following tasks –

- Manages the file system namespace.
- Regulates client's access to files.
- It also executes file system operations such as renaming, closing, and opening files and directories.

DataNode:

The DataNode is commodity hardware, having the GNU/Linux operating system and DataNode software. For every node (Commodity hardware/System) in a cluster, there will be a DataNode. These nodes manage the data storage of their system.

- DataNode perform read-write operations on the file systems, as per client request.
- They also perform operations such as block creation, deletion, and replication according to the instructions of the NameNode.

Block:

The user data is stored in the files of HDFS. The file in a file system will be divided into one or more segments and stored in individual data nodes. These file segments are called blocks. In other words, the minimum amount of data that HDFS can read or write is called a Block. The default block size is 64MB, but it can be increased as per the need to change in HDFS configuration.

Features of GFS:

- GFS was designed for high fault tolerance.
- Master and chunk servers can be restarted in a few seconds, each chunk is replicated at least three places and can tolerate at least two data crashes for a single chunk of data.

- The shadow master handles the failure of the GFS master.
- For data integrity, GFS makes checksums on every 64KB block in each chunk.
- GFS can achieve the goals of high availability, high performance, and implementation.

Features of HDFS:

- **Cost-effective:**

In <u>HDFS architecture</u>, the DataNodes, which store the actual data are inexpensive commodity hardware, thus reduces storage costs.

- **Large Datasets/ Variety and volume of data:**

HDFS can store data in any size and format (structured, unstructured).

- **Replication:**

Data Replication is one of the most important and unique features of HDFS. In HDFS, replication of data solves the problem of data loss in unfavorable conditions. The data is replicated across several machines in the cluster by creating replicas of blocks. The process of replication is maintained at regular intervals by HDFS.

- **High Availability:**

The High availability feature of Hadoop ensures the availability of data even during NameNode or DataNode failure.

- **High Throughput:**

Hadoop HDFS stores data in a distributed fashion, which allows data to be processed parallel on a cluster of nodes. This decreases the processing time and thus provides high throughput.

COMPARISON BETWEEN GFS AND HDFS
Properties
GFS
HDFS
Design Goals

- The main goal of GFS is to support large files
- Used for data-intensive computing.
- Store data reliably, even when failures occur within chunk servers, master, or network partitions.
- GFS is designed more for batch processing rather than interactive use by users.

- One of the main goals of HDFS is to support large files.
- Used for data-intensive computing.
- Store data reliably, even when failures occur within name nodes, data nodes, or network partitions.
- HDFS is designed more for batch processing rather than interactive use by users.

Processes

- Master and chunk server

- Name node and Data node

File Management

- Files are organized hierarchically in directories and identified by path names.
- GFS is exclusively for Google only.

- HDFS supports a traditional hierarchical file organization.
- HDFS also supports third-party file systems such as Cloud Store and Amazon Simple Storage Service.

Security

- Google has dozens of data centers for redundancy. These data centers are in undisclosed locations and most are unmarked for protection.
- Access is allowed to authorized employees and vendors only.

- HDFS security is based on the POSIX model of users and groups.
- Security is limited to simple file permissions.

Database Files

- Bigtable is the database used by GFS. Bigtable is a proprietary distributed database of Google Inc.

- HBase provides Bigtable (Google)-like capabilities on top of Hadoop Core.

File Serving

- A file in GFS is comprised of fixed-sized chunks. The size of the chunk is 64MB.

- HDFS is divided into large blocks for storage and access, typically 64MB in size.

Cache Management

- Clients do cache metadata.
- Neither the server nor the client caches the file data.
- Chunks are stored as local files in a Linux system.

- HDFS uses distributed cache
- It is a facility provided by the Map-Reduce framework to cache application-specific, large, read-only files (text, archives, jars, and so on)
- Private and Public Distributed Cache Files.

Communication

- TCP connections are used for communication. Pipelining is used for data transfer over TCP connections.

- RPC based protocol on top of TCP/IP

BIG TABLE

- Cloud Bigtable is a sparsely populated table that can scale to billions of rows and thousands of columns, enabling you to store terabytes or even petabytes of data. A single value in each row is indexed; this value is known as the row key.

- Cloud Bigtable is ideal for storing very large amounts of single-keyed data with very low latency. It supports high read and writes throughput at low latency, and it is an ideal data source for Map-Reduce operations.
- Cloud Bigtable is exposed to applications through multiple client libraries, including a supported extension to the Apache HBase library for Java.

Cloud Bigtable's powerful back-end servers offer several key advantages over a self-managed HBase installation:

- **Incredible scalability** - Cloud Bigtable scales in direct proportion to the number of machines in your cluster. A self-managed HBase installation has a design bottleneck that limits the performance after a certain threshold is reached. Cloud Bigtable does not have this bottleneck to scale the cluster up to handle more reads and writes.
- **Simple administration** - Cloud Bigtable handles upgrades and restarts transparently. It automatically maintains high data durability. To replicate data, simply add a second cluster to an instance, and replication starts automatically. No more managing replicas or regions; just design the table schemas, and Cloud Bigtable will handle.
- **Cluster resizing without downtime** - Increase the size of a Cloud Bigtable cluster for a few hours to handle a large load, and then reduce the cluster's size again—all without any downtime. After changing a cluster's size, it typically takes just a few minutes under load for Cloud Bigtable to balance performance across all of the nodes in the cluster.

HBASE AND DYNAMO

HBase is a data model that is similar to Google's big table designed to provide quick random access to huge amounts of structured data.

Architecture:

Figure 3.3 HBase – Architecture

Master Server:

The master server -

- Assigns regions to the region servers and takes the help of Apache Zoo Keeper for this task.
- Handles load balancing of the regions across region servers. It unloads the busy servers and shifts the regions to less occupied servers.
- Maintains the state of the cluster by negotiating the load balancing.
- Is also responsible for schema changes and other metadata operations such as creation of tables and

column families.

Regions:

Regions are nothing but tables that are split up and spread across the region servers.

Region server:

The region servers have regions that -

- Communicate with the client and handle data-related operations.
- Handle read and write requests for all the regions under it.
- Decide the size of the region by following the region size thresholds.

Regional Server

Figure 3.4 Regions and Stores

The store contains a memory store and HFiles. Memstore is just like a cache memory. Anything that is entered into the HBase is stored here initially. Later, the data is transferred and saved in Hfiles as blocks and the memstore is flushed.

Zookeeper

- Zookeeper is an open-source project that provides services like maintaining configuration information, naming, providing distributed synchronization, etc.
- Zookeeper has ephemeral nodes representing different region servers. Master servers use these nodes to discover available servers.
- In addition to availability, the nodes are also used to track server failures or network partitions.
- Clients communicate with region servers via zookeeper.
- In pseudo and standalone modes, HBase itself will take care of the zookeeper.

MAP-REDUCE AND EXTENSIONS: PARALLEL COMPUTING

- The Map-Reduce programming model was developed at Google in the process of implementing large-scale search and text processing tasks on massive collections of web data stored using BigTable and the GFS distributed file system.
- The Map-Reduce programming model is designed for processing and generating large volumes of data via massively parallel computations.
- The underlying infrastructure to support this model needs to assume that processors and networks will fail, even during a particular computation, and build in support for handling such failures while ensuring the progress of the computations being performed.

Parallel Computing

Parallel computing is the use of multiple processing elements simultaneously for solving any problem. Problems are broken down into instructions and are solved concurrently as each resource that has been applied to work is working at the same time.

Advantages of Parallel Computing:

- It saves time and money as many resources working together will reduce the time and cut potential costs.
- It can be impractical to solve larger problems on Serial Computing.
- It can take advantage of non-local resources when the local resources are finite.
- Serial Computing 'wastes' the potential computing power, thus Parallel Computing makes better work of the hardware.

Types of Parallelism:

- **Bit-level parallelism:** It is the form of parallel computing which is based on the increasing processor's size. It reduces the number of instructions that the system must execute to perform a task on large-sized data.
- **Instruction-level parallelism:** A processor can only address less than one instruction for each clock cycle phase. These instructions can be re-ordered and grouped which are later on executed concurrently without affecting the result of the program.
- **Task Parallelism:** Task parallelism employs the decomposition of a task into subtasks and then allocating each of the subtasks for execution. The processors perform the execution of sub-tasks

concurrently.

Applications of Parallel Computing:

- Databases and Data mining.
- Real-time simulation of systems.
- Science and Engineering.
- Advanced graphics, augmented reality, and virtual reality.

Limitations of Parallel Computing:

- It addresses such as communication and synchronization between multiple sub-tasks and processes which is difficult to achieve.
- The algorithms must be managed in such a way that they can be handled in the parallel mechanism.
- The algorithms or program must have low coupling and high cohesion. But it's difficult to create such programs.
- More technically skilled and expert programmers can code a parallelism based program well.

THE MAP-REDUCE MODEL

Map-Reduce is a processing technique and a program model for distributed computing based on java. The Map-Reduce algorithm contains two important tasks, namely Map and Reduce. The map takes a set of data and converts it into another set of data, where individual elements are broken down into tuples.

Figure 3.5 Map-Reduce Model

- **Parallel efficiency of map-reduce :**

Map-Reduce is the preferred cloud computing framework used in large data analysis and application processing. Map-Reduce frameworks currently in place suffer performance degradation due to the adoption of sequential processing approaches with little modification and thus exhibit underutilization of cloud resources.

RELATIONAL OPERATIONS

In relational algebra first need to know what a relation represents. As familiar with SQL there is no point in putting a long description here. A relation represents a database table. A major point that distinguishes SQL and relational algebra are that in relational algebra duplicate rows are implicitly eliminated which is not the case with SQL implementations.

- **Selection:** The SELECT operation is used for selecting a subset of the tuples according to a given selection condition.
- **Projection:** The projection operator helps to select some columns only in given table. It's analogous to SELECT in

SQL.

Image for post

Image for post

Figure 3.6 Selection operations Figure 3.7 Projection operations

- **Union:**It concatenates two tables vertically. Similar to UNION in SQL, but the duplicate rows are removed implicitly. The point to note in the below output table is that (Smith, 16) was a duplicate row so it appears only once in the output whereas (Tom, 17), (Tom, 19) appears as two, as those are not identical rows.
- **Intersection:** Same as INTERSECT in SQL. It intersects two tables and selects only the common rows.

Image for post

Image for post

Figure 3.8 Union the two tables Figure 3.9 Intersection of two tables

- **Difference:** The rows that are in the first table but not in second are selected for output. That (Monty, 21) is not considered in the output as its present in the second table but not in first.
- **Natural Join:** Merge two tables based on some common column. It represents the INNER JOIN in SQL. But the condition is implicit on the column that is common in both tables. The output will only contain rows for which the values in the common column match. It will generate one row for every time the column value across two tables match as is the case below for Tom.

Image for post

Image for post

Figure 3.10 Difference between the two tables Figure 3.11 Natural Join

- **Grouping and Aggregation:** Group rows based on some set of columns and apply some aggregation (sum, count, max, min, etc.) on some columns of the small groups that are formed. This corresponds to GROUP BY in SQL.

Image for post

Figure 3.12 Group by Name and take sum of the Winning

ENTERPRISE BATCH PROCESSING

Enterprise applications contain tasks that can be executed without user interaction. These tasks are executed periodically or when resource usage is low, and they often process large amounts of information such as-log files, database records, or images. Examples include billing, report generation, data format conversion, and image processing.

Batch processing refers to running batch jobs on a computer system. Java EE includes a batch processing framework that provides the batch execution infrastructure common to all batch applications, enabling developers to concentrate on the business logic of their batch applications.

EXAMPLE/APPLICATIONS OF MAP REDUCE

- **Social Networks:**

Social networking users like Facebook, Twitter, and LinkedIn connect with friends and the community.

- **Entertainment:**

To discover the most popular movies Netflix uses Hadoop and Map-Reduce. This is the best solution and suggestions for registered users taking into account their interests.

Map-Reduce can determine how users are watching movies, analyzing their logs and clicks.

- **Electronic Commerce:**

E-commerce providers, such as Amazon, Wal-Mart, and eBay, use the Map-Reduce programming model to identify favorite products based on users' interests or buying behavior.

- **FraudDetection:**

Hadoop and Map-Reduce are used in the financial industries, including companies such as banks, insurance providers, and payment locations for fraud detection, trend identification, or business metrics through transaction analysis.

- **Search and Advertisement Mechanisms:**

Advertisement mechanisms utilize it to analyze and understand search behavior, trends, and missing results for specific keywords. Google and Yahoo use Map-Reduce to understand users' behavior, such as popular searches for an event such as presidential elections.

CHAPTER FOUR

CLOUD SECURITY FUNDAMENTALS

Advance Cloud Computing

Unit-4

CLOUD SECURITY FUNDAMENTALS

Cloud computing security consists of a set of policies, controls, procedures and technologies that work together to protect cloud-based systems, data, and infrastructure. These security measures are configured to protect cloud data, support regulatory compliance and protect customer's privacy as well as setting authentication rules for individual users and devices.

Protection measures:

- No single person should accumulate all these privileges.

- A provider should deploy stringent security devices, restricted access control policies, and surveillance mechanisms to protect the physical integrity of the hardware.

- By enforcing security processes, the provider itself can prevent attacks that require physical access to the machines.

- The only way a system administrator would be able to gain physical access to a node running a customer's VM is by diverting this VM to a machine under his/her control, located outside the IaaS's security perimeter.
- The cloud computing platform must be able to confine the VM execution inside the perimeter and guarantee that at any point a system administrator with root privileges remotely logged to a machine hosting a VM cannot access its memory.
- TCG (trusted computing group), a consortium of an industry leader to identify and implement security measures at the infrastructure level proposes a set of hardware and software technologies to enable the construction of trusted platforms suggests the use of "remote attestation" (a mechanism to detect changes to the user's computers by authorized parties).

VULNERABILITY ASSESSMENT TOOL FOR CLOUD

- **Qualys** makes public cloud deployments are secure and compliant. Quays' continuous security platform enables customers to easily detect and identify vulnerable systems and apps, helping them better face the challenges of growing cloud workloads.
- **Proof point** focuses specifically on email, with cloud-only services tailored to both enterprises and small to medium-sized businesses. Not only does it make sure none of the bad stuff gets in, but it also protects any outgoing data.
- **Zscaler** calls its product the "Direct to Cloud Network," and like many of these products, boasts that it's much easier to deploy and can be much more cost-efficient than traditional appliance security.

- **Cipher Cloud** is here to secure all those other "as a service" products used, such as Salesforce, Chatter, Box, Office 365, Gmail, Amazon Web Services, and more.
- **Centrify** aims at identity management across several applications and devices. The main goal is to make users, employers, and customer's look-alike as a central area to be viewed and accessed through company policies. It gives an alarm when a person tries to sign in from on premise cloud software or cloud applications. It

PRIVACY AND SECURITY IN CLOUD
Privacy in cloud:

- One of the main concerns regarding the security and privacy in cloud computing is the protection of data.

Millions of users have stored up their important data on these clouds, which is what makes it riskier to secure each and every bit of information.

- In cloud computing, data security has become a serious issue different data is distributed in different storage devices and machines including PCs, servers and different mobile devices such as smart phones and wireless sensor networks.
- If the security and privacy in cloud computing is neglected, then the private information of each user is at risk, allowing easy cyber breaches to hack into the system and exploit any users' private storage data.

- Security and privacy in cloud computing needs to take action if users are to trust the system again.

Security in cloud:

- The cloud computing environment has various functions— some of the major ones involve data storage and computing.
- The data protection and its security regarding stored information of individual users, therefore many consumers use the cloud so much and that is exactly why it has prospered through its use of trustful functions.
- The cloud has become a very important tool for large scale purposes, such as for business and companies to prosper and on the lower scales where it is used by almost every individual as a necessary part of their everyday life.
- It makes sense why a lot of people are fond of using it and are willing to trust the cloud system with their valuable information. But a data breach may break this trust. Therefore it is extremely crucial that the security and privacy in cloud computing must create a solid line of defense against these cyber-attacks.

CLOUD COMPUTING SECURITY ARCHITECTURE

Cloud security starts with cloud security architecture. An organization should first understand its current cloud security posture, and then plan the controls and cloud security solutions it will use to prevent and mitigate threats.

This planning is critical to secure hyper-complex environments, which may include multiple public clouds, SaaS and PaaS services, on premise resources, all of which are accessed from both corporate and unsecured personal devices.

The cloud security architecture model is usually expressed in terms of:

- **Security controls:** It includes technologies and processes. Controls should take into account the location of each Service Company, cloud provider, or third party.
- **Trust boundaries:** The different services and components deployed on the cloud
- **Standard interfaces and security protocols:** Such as SSL, IPsec, SFTP, LDAPS, SSH, SCP, SAML, OAuth, etc.)
- **Techniques used for token management:** Authentication and authorization
- **Encryption methods:** Including algorithms like 128-bit AES, Triple DES, RSA, and Blowfish.
- **Security event logging:** Ensuring all relevant security events are captured, prioritized, and delivered to security teams.

The security services consumed by the cloud application:

- Logical location: Protocol
- Service function: Input/output
- Control description
- Actor

Figure 4.1: Cloud Security Architecture

ARCHITECTURAL CONSIDERATIONS- GENERAL ISSUES

The following table illustrates the dependencies which should be taken into consideration when architecting security controls into applications for cloud deployments:

Public/Hybrid Cloud –Threats

Private Cloud -Threats

Mitigation

IaaS

- OWASP Top 10
- Data leakage (inadequate ACL)
- Privilege escalation via management console mis-configuration
- Exploiting VM weakness
- DoS attack via API

- Weak protection of privileged keys
- VM Isolation failure

- OWASP Top 10
- Data theft (insiders)
- Privilege escalation via management console mis-configuration

- Testing apps and API for OWASP Top 10 vulnerabilities
- Hardening of VM image
- Security controls including encryption, multi-factor authentication, fine granular authorization, logging
- Security automation - Automatic provisioning of firewall policies, privileged accounts, DNS, application identity

PaaS

- Privilege escalation via API
- Authorization weakness in platform services such as Message Queue, NoSQL, Blob services
- Vulnerabilities in the run time engine resulting in tenant isolation failure

- Privilege escalation via API

Table 4.1: Architectural dependencies
TRUSTED CLOUD COMPUTING

Trusted computing is a broad term that refers to technologies and proposals for resolving computer security problems through hardware enhancements and associated software modifications. Several major hardware manufacturers and software vendors, collectively known as the Trusted Computing Group (TCG), are cooperating in this venture and have come up with specific plans.

The TCG develops and promotes specifications for the protection of computer resources from threats posed by malicious entities without infringing on the rights of end-users. Microsoft defines trusted computing by breaking it down into four technologies, all of which require the use of new or improved hardware at the personal computer (PC) level:

- Memory curtaining -- prevents programs from inappropriately reading from or writing to each other's memory.
- Secure input/output (I/O) -- addresses threats from spyware such as key loggers and programs that capture the contents of a display.
- Sealed storage -- allows computers to securely store encryption keys and other critical data.
- Remote attestation -- detects unauthorized changes to software by generating encrypted certificates for all applications on a PC.

To be effective, these measures must be supported by advances and refinements in the software and operating systems (OSs) that PCs use.

The trusted computing base (TCB) encompasses everything in a computing system that provides a secure environment. This includes the OS and its standard security mechanisms, computer hardware, physical locations, network resources, and prescribed procedures.

The term trusted PC refers to the industry ideal of a PC with built-in security mechanisms that place minimal reliance on the end-user to keep the machine and its peripheral devices secure. The intent is that, once effective mechanisms are built into the hardware, computer security will be less dependent on the vigilance of individual users and network administrators than it has historically been.

CLOUD COMPUTING SECURITY CHALLENGES

- **DDOS and DDoS attacks:** A DDoS attack is designed to overwhelm website servers so it can no longer respond to legitimate user requests.

If a DDoS attack is successful, it renders a website useless for hours, or even days. This can result in a loss of revenue, customer trust and brand authority.

- **Data breaches:** Data breaches can be the main goal of an attack through which sensitive information such as health, financial, personal identity, intellectual, and other related information is viewed, stolen, or used by an unauthorized user.
- **System vulnerability:** Security breaches may occur due to exploitable bugs in programs that stay within a system. This allows a bad actor to infiltrate and get access to sensitive information or crash the service operations.
- **Account or service hijacking using stolen passwords:** Account or service hijacking can be done to gain access and abuse highly privileged accounts. Attack methods like fraud, phishing, and exploitation of software vulnerability are carried out mostly using the stolen passwords.
- **Data loss:** The data loss threat occurs in the cloud due to interaction with risks within the cloud or architectural characteristics of the cloud application. Unauthorized

parties may access data to delete or alter records of an organization.

- **Shared technology vulnerabilities:** Cloud providers deliver their services by sharing applications, or infrastructure. Sometimes, the components that make up the infrastructure for cloud technology-as-a-service offers are not designed to offer strong isolation properties for a multi-tenant cloud service.

Risks to Cloud Environments:

- **Isolation failure:** Multi-tenancy and shared resources are defining characteristics of cloud computing. This risk category covers the failure of mechanisms separating storage, memory, routing, and reputation between different tenants.

It should be considered that attacks on resource isolation mechanisms are still less numerous and much more difficult for an attacker to put in practice compared to attacks on traditional OSs.

- **Management interface compromise:** Customer management interfaces of a public cloud provider are accessible through the Internet and mediate access to larger sets of resources (than traditional hosting providers) and therefore pose an increased risk, especially when combined with remote access and web browser vulnerabilities.
- **Data protection:** Cloud computing poses several data protection risks for cloud customers and providers. In some cases, it may be difficult for the cloud customer (in its role as data controller) to effectively check the

data handling practices of the cloud provider and thus to be sure that the data is handled lawfully.

- **Malicious insider:** while usually less likely, the damage which may be caused by malicious insiders is often far greater. Cloud architectures necessitate certain roles which are extremely high-risk. Examples include CP system administrators and managed security service providers.

Overcoming Challenges in Cloud Computing:

1. **Security and Privacy:** Security is arguably the biggest challenge in cloud computing. Cloud security refers to a set of technologies or policies to protect data. Remember, violating privacy can cause havoc to end-users.

- Implementing security applications, encrypted file systems, and data loss software to prevent attacks on cloud infrastructures.
- Using security tools and adopting a corporate culture that upholds data security discreetly.

1. **Cloud Costs:** Costing is a significant challenge in the adoption, migration, and operation of cloud computing services, especially for small and medium-sized businesses.

- Prepare a cost estimate budget right from the start. It involves experts who will help for cloud cost management. An additional measure is creating a centralized team to oversee budget details.

3. **Reliability and Availability:** cloud providers continue to improve their uptimes; service disruption is still an enrollment problem. Small-scale cloud service providers are more prone to downtime. This problem persists today even with well-developed backups and platform advancements.

- Cloud computing service providers have resorted to creating multiple redundancy levels in their systems. Also, they are developing disaster recovery setups and backup plans to mitigate outages.

VIRTUALIZATION SECURITY MANAGEMENT

- **Migration management:** VM migration is easy to attack and is a vulnerable process. Special security mechanisms should be applied when a VM is migrated from a place to somewhere else. It sounds like an easy process but it is not.

When any of the organizations or an enterprise tries to use any of the automated tools such as live migration many other factors creep in. Two different VMs on a single machine may cause a violation to Payment Card Industry (PCI).

- **VM Image Management:** VM Image (VMI) is a type of file or the format of the data which is used to create the virtual machine in the environment of virtualization. Hence, the confidential data and the integrity of VMIs are very important when the VMs are migrating or starting.

- **Patch Management:** Patch management is acquiring, installing, or testing system management or inserting code changes to the computer system administration. It also includes on the available patches of the maintaining current knowledge ensuring the patches are installed properly. Patch management is built for identify and test the various types of code changes.
- **Audit:** In the lifecycle of the Virtual machines, the sensitive data and the behavior of the virtual machines should be monitored throughout the virtual system. This may be done with auditing which provides the mechanism to check the traces of the activities left by the virtual system.

VIRTUAL THREATS

Some of the virtual threats to Cloud computing security are:

1. Shared clipboard:

Shared clipboard technologies enable information to become transferred between VMs as well as the host, offering a means of moving information between malicious programs in VMs of various security realms.

2. Keystroke logging:

Some VM technologies allow the logging of keystrokes and screen updates to become passed across virtual terminals within the virtual machine, writing to host files and permitting the monitoring of encrypted terminal connections in the VM.

3. VM monitoring in the host:

Since all network packets coming from or planning to a VM pass with the host, the host may be able to impact the VM from the following this:

- Starting, stopping, pausing, and restart VMs
- Monitoring and configuring resources available to the VMs, including CPU, memory, disk, and network usage of VMs
- Adjusting the amount of CPUs, level of memory, quantity, and variety of virtual disks, and quantity of virtual network interfaces offered to a VM.
- Monitoring the applications running inside the VM.
- The viewing, copying, and modifying data stored about the VM's virtual disks.

4. Virtual machine monitoring from another VM:

VMs shouldn't have the ability to directly access one another's virtual disks around the host. Nevertheless, if the VM platform uses a virtual hub or switches for connecting the VMs to the host, then intruders may be able to use a hacker technique called "ARP poisoning" to redirect packets planning to or in the other VM for sniffing.

5. Virtual machine backdoors:

Virtual machine backdoors, covert communications channel between guest and host could allow intruders to execute potentially harmful operations.

VM SECURITY RECOMMENDATIONS

Following virtual machine security recommendations help ensure the integrity of the cloud:

- **General Virtual Machine Protection:** A virtual machine is, in most respects, the equivalent of a physical server. Employ the same security measures in virtual machines that for physical systems.
- **Minimize Use of the Virtual Machine Console:** The virtual machine console provides the same function for a virtual machine that a monitor provides on a physical

server.

Users with access to the virtual machine console have access to virtual machine power management and removable device connectivity controls. Console access might therefore allow a malicious attack on a virtual machine.

- **Prevent Virtual Machines from Taking over Resources:** When one virtual machine consumes so much of the host resources that other virtual machines on the host cannot perform their intended functions, a Denial of Service (DoS) might occur.

To prevent a virtual machine from causing a DoS, use host resource management features such as setting Shares and using resource pools.

- **Disable Unnecessary Functions Inside Virtual Machines:** Any service that is running in a virtual machine provides the potential for attack. By disabling system components that are not necessary to support the application or service that is running on the system, to reduce the potential.

VM-SPECIFIC SECURITY TECHNIQUES

- **Protecting the VMM:**

A hypervisor can be used to monitor the virtualized systems it is hosting. However, the hypervisor can in turn be targeted and modified by an attack. As the hypervisor possesses every privilege on its guest systems, it is crucial to preserve its integrity. However, while it is possible to ensure the integrity of a system during boot it is much harder to ensure runtime integrity.

To ensure runtime integrity, one could think of installing a second hypervisor under the initial hypervisor dedicated to monitoring it, similar to one would have to guarantee that the most privileged hypervisor cannot, in turn, be corrupted. Several studies have therefore focused on using other means to ensure the integrity of the most privileged element.

• **Protecting the VMs against their VMM:**

The purpose of CloudVisor is to ensure data confidentiality and integrity for the VM, even if some elements of the virtualization system (hypervisor, management VM, another guest VM) are compromised. The idea is that data belonging to a VM but accessed by something else than this VM appears encrypted.

• **Virtual Machine Encryption:**

A virtual machine consists of a set of files, machine theft has now become much easier. Furthermore, stealing a virtual machine can be achieved with relative ease by simply snap shooting the VM and copying the snap shorted files.

• **Encryption under the hypervisor:**

VMs can be encrypt the hypervisor. By using standard protocols such as NFS or iSCSI, the encryption is independent of the hypervisor platform. That means hypervisor features such as VMotion and LiveMigration continue to work unchanged. As VMs are copied into an encrypted data store, they will be encrypted according to the encryption policy.

- **Encryption within the VM:**

In this model, for all devices encrypted, there is an encrypted path from the VM's operating system through the hypervisor and down to the storage layer. This prevents VM administrators from being able to view sensitive data that resides within the VM. In this environment, as with the previous one described, the key server could reside anywhere.

- **Encryption of VM images and application data:**

Another model combines encryption at the VM and storage layers. This combined option is superior because there's an encrypted path for sensitive data from the VM through the hypervisor. This prevents the VM administrator from seeing clear text data.

SECURE EXECUTION ENVIRONMENTS AND COMMUNICATIONS IN CLOUD

- An Execution Environment is an environment for executing code, in which those executing the code can have high levels of trust in that surrounding environment because it can ignore threats from the rest of the device.

Execution Environment stands and distinguishes them from the uncertain nature of applications. Generally, the rest of the device hosts a feature Rich OS like Android, and so is generically known in this context as the REE (Rich Operating System Execution Environment).

- Cloud communications are the blending of multiple communication modalities. These include methods such as voice, email, chat, and video, in an integrated fashion to reduce or eliminate communication lag. Cloud communications are essentially internet-based communication.
- Cloud communications evolved from data to voice with the introduction of VoIP (voice over Internet Protocol). A branch of cloud communication is cloud telephony, which refers specifically to voice communications
- Cloud communications providers host communication services through servers that they own and maintain. The customers, in turn, access these services through the cloud and only pay for services that they use, doing away with maintenance associated with PBX (private branch exchange) system deployment.

The need for cloud communications has resulted from the following trends in the enterprise:

- Distributed and decentralized company operations in branch and home offices
- Increase in the number of communication and data devices accessing the enterprise networks
- Hosting and managing IT assets and applications

These trends have forced many enterprises to seek external services and to outsource their requirement for IT and communications. The cloud is hosted and managed by a third party, and the enterprise pays for and uses space on the cloud for its requirements. This has allowed enterprises to save on costs incurred for hosting and managing data storage and communication on their own.

The following are some of the communication and application products available under cloud communications that an enterprise can utilize:

- Private branch exchange
- SIP Trucking
- Call center
- Fax services
- Interactive voice response
- Text messaging
- Voice broadcast

All of these services cover the various communication needs of an enterprise. These include customer relations, intra-, and inter-branch communication, inter-department memos, conference, call forwarding, and tracking services, operations center, and office communications hub.

Cloud communication is a center for all enterprise-related communication that is hosted, managed, and maintained by third-party service providers for a fee charged to the

CHAPTER FIVE

ISSUES IN CLOUD COMPUTING

Advance Cloud Computing

Unit-5

ISSUES IN CLOUD COMPUTING

Cloud Computing is Internet-based computing, where shared resources, software, and information are provided to computers and other devices on demand.

These are major issues in Cloud Computing:

1. **Privacy:**

   The user data can be accessed by the host company with or without permission. The service provider may access the data that is on the cloud at any point in time. They could accidentally or deliberately alter or even delete information.

2. **Compliance:**

   There are many regulations in places related data and hosting. To comply with regulations (Federal Information Security Management Act, Health Insurance Portability and Accountability Act) user may have to adopt deployment modes that are expensive.

3. **Security:**
   Cloud-based services involve third-party for storage and security. Can one assume that a cloud-based company will protect and secure one's data if one is using their services at a very low or for free, They may share user's information with others. Security presents a real threat to cloud.

4. **Sustainability:**
   This issue refers to minimizing the effect of cloud computing on environment. Citing the server's effects on the environmental effects of cloud computing, in areas where climate favors natural cooling and renewable electricity is readily available, the countries with favorable conditions, such as Finland, Sweden, and Switzerland are trying to attract cloud computing data centers.

5. **Abuse:**
   While providing cloud services, it should be ascertained that the client is not purchasing the services of cloud computing for nefarious purpose. A banking Trojan illegally used the popular Amazon service as a command and control channel that issued software updates and malicious instruction to PCs that were infected by the malware.

IMPLEMENTING REAL TIME APPLICATION

Cloud computing is enabling businesses to take advantage of the latest technologies without having to spend fortunes on costly software, hardware and IT services. Today, many businesses and companies have embraced cloud computing and they are using it in different ways. Here are some of the most common ways through which businesses are applying cloud computing.

- **Communication:**

Emails are some of the most popular communication methods that businesses and companies use today. This service is evolving at a very fast rate becoming more reliable and faster. Today, most businesses are always email campaigning clients and using emails to store important data about their customers. Through cloud computing, webmail clients can use cloud storage while providing analytics surrounding email data from any location globally. Companies are also using cloud-based SaaS apps to enable access to enterprise information instantly from any location. Ideally, cloud computing has made it easier for companies and businesses to executive internal processes smoothly.

- **Collaboration:**

Cloud computing has made it easier for employees, clients and businesses to collaborate with ease. Sharing files and documents has been made easier by cloud computing. This has enhanced connections that are easy and less time-consuming. Google Wave for instance enables users to create files then invite other users to edit, collaborate with the files or comment. Collaboration with cloud computing is the same as instant messaging. However, it provides complete, specific tasks that take just hours instead of months to accomplish.

- **Data storage:**

Businesses are using cloud computing solutions to store crucial data. Data store in a business or home computer can only be accessed when using that device. However, cloud computing enables to store and access data anytime, anywhere and from any device. This storage is also secure because user gets a unique password and username that ensures that only user can access files online as well as encryption of the data. There are several security layers for cloud storage and this makes it extremely difficult for hackers to access the data in the cloud. Virtual office Perhaps, the most popular among all <u>real-time applications of cloud computing</u> is the ability to rent software (i.e. SaaS) rather than use it. For instance, Google Docs can be used to run a virtual office.

QOS ISSUES IN CLOUD

Cloud computing must assure the best service level for users. Services outlined in the service-level agreements must include guarantees on round-the-clock availability, adequate resources, performance, and bandwidth. Any compromise on these guarantees could prove fatal for customers.

The decision to switch to cloud computing should not be based on the hype in the industry. A good understanding of the technology enables the user to make smarter decisions. Knowing all the features will empower the business users to understand and negotiate with the Service Providers in a proactive manner.

- Workload modeling involves the assessment or prediction of the arrival rates of requests and of the demand for resources (e.g., CPU requirements) placed by applications on an infrastructure or platform, and the QoS observed in response to such workloads.
- System modeling aims at evaluating the performance of a cloud system, either at design time or at runtime.

Models are used to predict the value of specific QoS metrics such as response time, reliability or availability. We survey in formalisms and tools employed for these analyses and their current applications to assess the performance of cloud systems.

- Applications of QoS models often appear in relation to decision-making problems in system management. Techniques to determine optimized decisions range from simple heuristics to nonlinear programming and meta-heuristics. We survey in Section 4 works on decision making for capacity allocation, load balancing, and admission control including research works that provide solutions for the management of a cloud infrastructure (i.e., from the cloud provider perspective) and resource management techniques for the infrastructure user (e.g., an application provider aiming at minimizing operational expenditure, while providing QoS level guarantees to the end users).

DEPENDABILITY

Dependability is one of the highly crucial issues in cloud computing environments given the serious impact of failures on user experience. Cloud computing is a complex system based on virtualization and large scalability, which makes it a frequent place for failure. In order to fight against failures in a cloud, we assure dependability differently from the common way where the focus of fault management is on the Infrastructure as a Service and on the cloud provider side only.

DATA MIGRATION

Data migration is referred to as the process of transferring data from one location to another new and improved system or location. It effectively selects, prepares and transforms data to permanently transfer it from one system storage to another. With the focus of enterprises increasing on optimization and technological advancements, they are availing <u>database migration services</u> to move from their on-premises infrastructure to cloud-based storage and applications.

Types of data migration

- **Cloud Migration:** It is the process of moving data, applications and all important business elements from on premise data center to the cloud, or from one cloud to another.
- **Application Migration:** Involves transfer of application programs to a modern environment. It may move an entire application system from on premise IT center to the cloud or between clouds.
- **Storage Migration:** It is the process of moving data to a modern system from outdated arrays. It enhances the performance while offering cost-effective scaling.

STREAMING IN CLOUD

Streaming data is data that is generated continuously by thousands of data sources, which typically send in the data records simultaneously, and in small sizes (order of Kilobytes). Streaming data includes a wide variety of data such as log files generated by customers using mobile or web applications, ecommerce purchases, in-game player activity, information from social networks, financial trading floors, or geospatial services, and telemetry from connected devices or instrumentation in data centers.

This data needs to be processed sequentially and incrementally on a record-by-record basis or over sliding time windows, and used for a wide variety of analytics including correlations, aggregations, filtering, and sampling. Information derived from such analysis gives companies visibility into many aspects of their business and customer activity such as - service usage (for metering/billing), server activity, website clicks, and geo-location of devices, people, and physical goods and enables them to respond promptly to emerging situations.

Examples of streaming data

- Sensors in transportation vehicles, industrial equipment, and farm machinery send data to a streaming application. The application monitors performance, detects any potential defects in advance, and places a spare part order automatically preventing equipment down time.
- A financial institution tracks changes in the stock market in real time, computes value-at-risk, and automatically rebalances portfolios based on stock price movements.
- A real-estate website tracks a subset of data from consumers' mobile devices and makes real-time property recommendations of properties to visit based on their geo-location.

CLOUD MIDDLEWARE

Software that connects computers and devices to other applications. It can also be referred to as the slash or connecting point in client/server. Another way to define middleware is to say that it is software that acts as a liaison between applications and networks. The term is often used in the context of cloud computing, such as public or private cloud.

Middleware definition is to say that it acts as an intermediary. It is often used to support complicated and distributed applications. It can be a web server, application server, content management system, or other tool that supports application development and delivery. It can also be a software application that connects two or more applications so that data can be shared between them.

Types of Middleware

- **Message Oriented Middleware:** Message oriented middleware is a concept that involves the passing of data between applications using a communication channel that carries self-contained units of information (messages). In a MOM-based communication environment, messages are usually sent and received asynchronously.
- **Object Middleware:** Object-based middleware is runtime software that enables objects (components) to work cooperatively with a container program or another object, even if the software is distributed across multiple computers.
- **Remote Procedure Call (RPC) Middleware:** Remote procedure call (RPC) is a protocol that one program can use to request a service from a program located in another computer on a network without having to understand the network's details. A procedure call is also sometimes known as a function call or a subroutine call.
- **Database Middleware:** It connects two applications together so data and databases can be easily passed between the "pipe". Using middleware allows users to perform such requests as submitting forms on a web browser or allowing the web server to return dynamic

web pages based on a user's profile.

MOBILE CLOUD COMPUTING

<u>Mobile Cloud Computing</u> which is defined as a combination of mobile computing, cloud computing, and wireless network that come up together purpose such as rich computational resources to mobile users, network operators, as well as to cloud computing providers. Mobile Cloud Computing is meant to make it possible for rich mobile applications to be executed on a different number of mobile devices. In this technology, data processing, and data storage happen outside of mobile devices. Mobile Cloud Computing applications leverage this IT architecture to generate the following advantages:

1. Extended battery life.
2. Improvement in data storage capacity and processing power.
3. Improved synchronization of data due to "store in one place, accessible from anywhere" platform theme.
4. Improved reliability and scalability.
5. Ease of integration.

Characteristics of Mobile Cloud Computing Application

1. <u>**Cloud infrastructure**</u>: Cloud infrastructure is a specific form of information architecture that is used to store data.
2. **Data cache:**The data can be locally cached.
3. **User Accommodation:**Scope of accommodating different user requirements in cloud app development is available in mobile Cloud Computing.

4. **Easy Access:** It is easily accessed from desktop or mobile devices alike.
5. **Cloud Apps:** facilitate to provide access to a whole new range of services.

INTER CLOUD ISSUES

Inter cloud or 'cloud of clouds' is a term refer to a theoretical model for cloud computing services based on the idea of combining many different individual clouds into one seamless mass in terms of on-demand operations.

- **Security issues:** Cloud-based services involve third-party for storage and security. Can one assume that a cloud-based company will protect and secure one's data if one is using their services at a very low or for free? They may share user's information with others. Security presents a real threat to cloud.
- **Lack of resources/expertise:** As the usage of cloud technologies is increasing, tools to manage it are getting sophisticated, finding experts on top of this in cloud computing is becoming a bottleneck to many organizations. Many companies are adopting automated cloud management technologies but it's always better to train individuals to satisfy the need of time.
- **Performance:** Cloud Computing is on-demand compute service and supports multitenancy, thus performance should not suffer over the acquisition of new users. The CSP should maintain enough resources to serve all the users and any ad-hoc requests.

A GRID OF CLOUDS

Grid computing is a group of networked computers which work together as a virtual supercomputer to perform large tasks, such as analyzing huge sets of data or weather modeling. They use computers which are part of the grid only when idle and operators can perform tasks unrelated to the grid at any time.

1) **Computational Grid:** A computational grid is a loose network of computers linked to perform grid computing. In a computational grid, a large computational task is divided up among individual machines, which run calculations in parallel and then return results to the original computer.

2) **Data Grid:** A data grid is an architecture or set of services that gives individuals or groups of users the ability to access, modify and transfer extremely large amounts of geographically distributed data for research purposes.

3) **Collaborative Grid:** In grid computing, resources are used in collaborative pattern, and also in grid computing, the users do not pay for use. ... In cloud computing, resources are used in centralized pattern. While in grid computing, resources are used in collaborative pattern.

Grid Characteristics

- **Large scale:** A grid must be able to deal with a number of resources ranging from just a few to millions. This raises the very serious problem of avoiding potential performance degradation as the grid size increases.
- **Geographical distribution:** Grid's resources may be located at distant places.
- **Heterogeneity:** A grid hosts both software and hardware resources that can be very varied ranging from data, files, software components or programs to sensors, scientific instruments, display devices, personal digital organizers, computers, super-computers and networks.

- **Resource sharing:** Resources in a grid belong to many different organizations that allow other organizations (i.e. users) to access them. Nonlocal resources can thus be used by applications, promoting efficiency and reducing costs.
- **Multiple administrations:** Each organization may establish different security and administrative policies under which their owned resources can be accessed and used. As a result, the already challenging network security problem is complicated even more with the need of taking into account all different policies.

SKY COMPUTING

Sky Computing is an emerging computing model where resources from multiple clouds providers are leveraged to create large scale distributed infrastructures.

Figure 5.1 Sky Computing

- Sky computing allows users to control resources on their own. So trust relationships within sky computing are the same as those within a traditional non distributed site, simplifying how remote resources interact.

- It is dynamically scalable as resources are distributed over several cloud.
- Sky computing deploy a single appliance with a specific provider, we rely on basic security and contextualization measures this provider – specific networking & security context.
- To connects the client to a trusted networking domain and configures explicit trust & relationships between them so that client securely takes ownership of customized infrastructure for an agreed time period.
- Seasonal e-commerce web server, event based alert systems.

LOAD BALANCING

Cloud Load balancing is the process of distributing workloads and computing resources across one or more servers. This kind of distribution ensures maximum throughput in minimum response time. The workload is segregated among two or more servers, hard drives, network interfaces or other computing resources, enabling better resource utilization and system response time. Thus, for a high traffic website, effective use of cloud load balancing can ensure business continuity.

The common objectives of using load balancers are:

- To maintain system firmness.
- To improve system performance.
- To protect against system failures.

The advantages of Cloud Load Balancing

- **High Performing applications:** Cloud load balancing techniques, unlike their traditional on premise counterparts, are less expensive and simple to implement. Enterprises can make their client applications work faster and deliver better performances, that too at potentially lower costs.
- **Increased scalability:** Cloud balancing takes help of cloud's scalability and agility to maintain website traffic. By using efficient load balancers, can easily match up the increased user traffic and distribute it among various servers or network devices.
- **Ability to handle sudden traffic spikes:** A normally running University site can completely go down during any result declaration. This is because too many requests can arrive at the same time. If they are using cloud load balancers, they do not need to worry about such traffic surges. No matter how large the request is, it can be wisely distributed among different servers for generating maximum results in less response time.

RESOURCE OPTIMIZATION AND RESOURCE DYNAMIC RECONFIGURATION

Cloud optimization is the process of correctly selecting and assigning the right resources to a workload or application. When workload performance, compliance, and cost are correctly and continually balanced against the best-fit infrastructure in real time, efficiency is achieved.

A cloud configuration system provides the ability to dynamically reconfigure a set of computing resources to define a cloud into multiple separate logical cloud instances. The system includes a reconfiguration tool that reads an existing system and network configuration from a configuration store, allows the user to change the configuration into multiple logical systems, performs some syntactical checks, and stores the new configuration into the configuration store.

MONITORING IN CLOUD

Cloud monitoring is the process of evaluating, monitoring, and managing cloud-based services, applications, and infrastructure. Companies utilize various application monitoring tools to monitor cloud-based applications. Here's a look at how it works and best practices for success.

Types of cloud monitoring

- **Database monitoring:** Cloud applications rely on databases, this technique reviews processes, queries, availability, and consumption of cloud database resources. This technique can also track queries and data integrity, monitoring connections to show real-time usage data. For security purposes, access requests can be tracked as well.

- **Website monitoring:** A website is a set of files that is stored locally, which, in turn, sends those files to other computers over a network. This monitoring technique tracks processes, traffic, availability, and resource utilization of cloud-hosted sites.

- **Virtual machine monitoring:** This technique is a simulation of a computer within a computer; that is, virtualization infrastructure and virtual machines. It's usually scaled out in IaaS as a virtual server that hosts several virtual desktops.

Benefits of Cloud Monitoring

- Scaling for increased activity is seamless and works in organizations of any size.
- Dedicated tools (and hardware) are maintained by the host.
- Tools are used across several types of devices, including desktop computers, tablets, and phones, so organization can monitor apps from any location.
- Installation is simple because infrastructure and configurations are already in place.
- System doesn't suffer interruptions when local problems emerge, because resources are not part of organization's servers and workstations.
- Subscription-based solutions can keep user costs low.

INSTALLING CLOUD PLATFORMSAND PERFORMANCE EVALUATION

There are three major players in the public cloud platforms arena - Amazon Web Services (AWS), Microsoft's Azure, and Google Cloud Platform. The top cloud computing companies are addressing a large and growing market.

Performance analysis is a complex process, but the goal is very simple: to identify the root cause of a problem. Toward this end, we proceed in an orderly, step-by-step manner to home in on the fault domain containing the root cause. Since this chapter is specifically about virtualization and cloud computing, we'll discuss how those two domains affect this process. But first let's examine the high-level flow of a root-cause analysis.

We begin with a typical problem, slow application response time, then in step-by-step fashion, we'll narrow down the possibilities:

- Decide whether the problem affects the entire application, or just a particular transaction or transaction type. If the latter, then our first step is to isolate the transaction type that slows down. This will define the context for further investigation.
- Identify the problematic tier or tiers. The problem might lie between two tiers (i.e., due to network latency).
- To isolate the problem further, check whether the environment itself has a negative impact, such as CPU exhaustion, memory constraints. This would include anything that is external to the application itself; for instance garbage-collection suspensions.
- Finally, isolate the problem to a specific component, method, or service call within the application. From this point, we can determine if the root cause is algorithmic, CPU-centric, a result of excessive VM suspensions, or caused by external bottlenecks, such as I/O, network, or locks (synchronization).

FEATURES OF CLOUD COMPUTING PLATFORMS

- **Resources Pooling:** It means that the Cloud provider pulled the computing resources to provide services to multiple customers with the help of a multi-tenant model. There are different physical and virtual resources assigned and reassigned which depends on the demand of the customer.
- **On-Demand Self-Service:** It is one of the important and valuable features of Cloud Computing as the user can continuously monitor the server uptime, capabilities, and allotted network storage. With this feature, the user can also monitor the computing capabilities.

- **Easy Maintenance:** The servers are easily maintained and the downtime is very low and even in some cases, there is no downtime. Cloud Computing comes up with an update every time by gradually making it better.
- **Large Network Access:** The user can access the data of the cloud or upload the data to the cloud from anywhere just with the help of a device and an internet connection. These capabilities are available all over the network and accessed with the help of internet.
- **Availability:** The capabilities of the Cloud can be modified as per the use and can be extended a lot. It analyzes the storage usage and allows the user to buy extra cloud storage if needed for a very small amount.

FUNCTIONS OF CLOUD COMPUTING PLATFORMS

Cloud computing is the use of computing resources (hardware and software) that are delivered as a service over a network (typically the Internet). The name comes from the use of a cloud-shaped symbol as an abstraction for the complex infrastructure it contains in system diagrams. Cloud computing entrusts remote services with a user's data, software and computation.

As technology develops there is a need for companies and businesses to figure out how to use cloud computing for business improvements. This means boosting output while keeping costs down. For the smart business, cloud computing provides a unique critical success factor that if harnessed properly could allow a business to operate more cost effectively than the competition. Like most technologies, cloud computing streamlines operations, reduces their cost and reduces strain on resources like power while at the same time providing higher security.

- **Infrastructure-as-a-Service (IaaS):**Infrastructure-as-a-Service (IaaS) delivers fundamental compute, network, and storage resources to consumer's on-demand, over the internet, and on a pay-as-you-go basis. Using an existing infrastructure on a pay-per-use scheme seems to be an obvious choice for companies saving on the cost of investing to acquire, manage, and maintain an IT infrastructure.
- **Platform-as-a-Service (PaaS):** Platform-as-a-Service (PaaS) provides customers a complete platform—hardware, software, and infrastructure—for developing, running, and managing applications without the cost, complexity, and inflexibility of building and maintaining that platform on-premises. Organizations may turn to PaaS for the same reasons they look to IaaS, while also seeking to increase the speed of development on a ready-to-use platform to deploy applications.
- **Big data analytics:** One of the aspects offered by leveraging cloud computing is the ability to use big data analytics to tap into vast quantities of both structured and unstructured data to harness the benefit of extracting business value.
- **Cloud storage:** Cloud can offer you the possibility of storing your files and accessing, storing, and retrieving them from any web-enabled interface. The web services interfaces are usually simple. At any time and place, you have high availability, speed, scalability, and security for your environment.